VISUAL LITERACY

VISUAL LITERACY

A CONCEPTUAL APPROACH
TO GRAPHIC PROBLEM SOLVING

JUDITH WILDE
RICHARD WILDE

WATSON-GUPTILL PUBLICATIONS
NEW YORK

First published in 1991 in New York by Watson-Guptill Publications,
a division of BPI Communications, Inc.,
1515 Broadway, New York, N.Y. 10036

Library of Congress Cataloging-in-Publication Data

Wilde, Judith.
    Visual literacy : a conceptual approach to solving graphic
problems / by Judith Wilde and Richard Wilde.
        p.   cm.
    Includes index.
    ISBN 0-8230-5619-8 : $45.00
    1. Graphic arts—Study and teaching.   2. Visual communication—
Technique.   I. Wilde, Richard.   II. Title.
NC845.W55   1991
741.6—dc20   90-25613
                                                          CIP

Manufactured in Singapore

First printing, 1991

1 2 3 4 5 6 7 8 9 / 95 94 93 92 91

Designed by Richard Wilde and Judith Wilde

This book is dedicated to our students, who make us better at what we love to do, and to our children, Brandon and Trilby, who have been patient and understanding throughout this project.

CONTENTS

I was shocked when I read through Richard and Judith Wilde's *Visual Literacy*. And dismayed, too. Not because it's flawed in any way, but because it's *so smart*. If I were given these assignments, I'm certain I would be in deep trouble. The problems included in this, the Wildes' second volume of student projects, are taxing and intimidating—not for their students, but to me. When I was in school, I learned about graphic form separately from content. A marriage between the two was considered unholy, and wholly disapproved of. The exercises herein are brilliant because they bring together technique and concept as though they were never distinct. You might ask, however, isn't design valid on its own formal terms, or for its own sake? Of course, there is a virtue in formalism, but graphic design is not an independent art form. It's about interdependence and interrelatedness, and the Wildes' problems stress both.

I learned about conceptual thinking the hard way—on the job. I entered a design field that at the time was more interested in decoration than substance, and in which practitioners were content to recycle old tricks and conceits. Fortunately, I inherited the art directorship of the *New York Times* op-ed page, which had already established itself as the wellspring of contemporary conceptual illustration, where metaphor, allegory, and symbolism were employed to convey meaningful editorial ideas. My previous schooling and professional training had not prepared me for the thinking required by this illustration genre. If I had been taught through the exercises presented in this book, my skills might have been honed sooner—perhaps even better.

The problems herein have no right or wrong answers. Each requires that the student conjure multiple solutions that test the limits of perception and comprehension. These are the stepping stones to acute conceptual thinking. Indeed, the clever ways in which the problems have been designed invite questions, not answers. The graphic forms beckon the student to experiment; the physical limitations provide necessary, but not inviolable, parameters; the time constraint imposed on all assignments hones powers of concentration and adaptation; and the wide variety of problems—requiring solutions ranging from the typographic to the illustrative—suggests numerous approaches to visual communications, both in and out of the school environment.

Perhaps even more important, this approach does not speak down to the neophyte. Though the problems range from fundamental issues (such as color and shape exercises) to more sophisticated abstract concepts (notions of sound, death, etc.), they are all explained efficiently, *not* simplistically. Moreover, the student is never left in the dark regarding intent, probably the most significant aspect of the problem-solving process.

Even with all my years of professional experience, after reading the problems and seeing the wonderfully varied solutions, I've been introduced to a new way of thinking—not only about teaching, but also about the graphic issues I deal with every day. I guess it's never too late to learn, and *Visual Literacy* is an excellent place to start.

STEVEN HELLER
Senior Art Director,
The New York Times

For most people, learning the principles of effective visual communications is an intensely personal venture. Among the more curious and vexing predicaments is the fact that the necessary visual communications concepts cannot be taught directly. The study of various media and techniques offers a certain tangibility for direct study, of course, but there is very little practical knowledge that can be imparted regarding an *overall conceptual approach* to visual communications. It is therefore necessary to create conditions conducive to students' personal exploration and discovery of this knowledge.

For educators in the ever-changing visual communications field, understanding how to create these conditions is a formidable challenge. It is essential that assignments be both educationally sound and personally meaningful to the students, creating sufficient interest to open up the students to previously unexplored avenues of problem solving. Educators should never assume that a student's mere enrollment in design school will inherently constitute a serious interest in solving visual communications problems—this interest must be *developed,* through the employment of personally interesting and involving problems.

The concern, then, for design educators is to demystify the visual communications process while presenting it in an exciting and challenging way. The problems in this book are structured to achieve just that, serving as original strategies to prompt original results. Each assignment is designed to lead students away from traditional thought processes, away from traditional avenues of visual research, and away from "right" and "wrong" answers; faced with open-ended questions, many of them presented in the context of seemingly narrow parameters, students are forced to look inward for personal design solutions. In short, the necessary conditions for personal creative growth are established again and again.

The issues addressed by the problems in this book include the following: reevaluating a problem in personal terms; creating conditions for self-questioning by moving from the known to the unknown; encouraging the use of concepts to dictate techniques, instead of the other way around; discovering design principles, rather than directly learning or memorizing them; and discovering personal conceptual methods of problem solving. The problems were given to beginning students, not only to teach basic design fundamentals but also to encourage personal creative processes and self-reliance. The wide variety of solutions shown for each problem reflects the diversity of options and potential approaches presented by each problem. Because self-discovery is stressed as the primary goal, certain "deviant" but nonetheless worthwhile solutions are presented as well.

Most of the assignments ask for several solutions to a single problem, a condition that expands problem-solving repertoires, breaks down limitations, and reinforces the need to explore. By dedicating themselves to creating, say, twenty solutions to a single problem, rather than just one or two, students can come to realize that the potential number of successful solutions is infinite. The idea of *unlearning* comes into play here as well, prodding students to go beyond habitual, learned responses and thought processes, into the realm of a more instinctive, spontaneous approach.

Visual Literacy can be used to simulate this experience, and the book is formatted to this end. Readers are encouraged to consider and solve the given problems prior to reviewing the displayed solutions. Approaching the book in this manner will also allow readers to assess the solutions more meaningfully than if they had simply viewed the solutions in terms of their formal concerns.

This conceptual approach to visual problem solving embodies the quest for visual literacy. It is accompanied by a responsibility that must be embraced by visual communicators, for it can enrich our culture by increasing the level of visual literacy throughout our society. It is this approach—facing the unknown, armed with the tool of diligent and introspective questioning—that is the best hope for creating future generations of visually literate designers.

ACKNOWLEDGMENTS

Many people contributed to the completion of this project. We wish to thank some who deserve special recognition.

Our colleagues and associates provided advice and feedback. In particular, we are grateful to Silas Rhodes, for his wisdom, David Rhodes, for his support and encouragement, Dr. Thomas Nonn, for his trust and understanding, and Jack Endewelt, for his friendship, patience, and good advice in formulating the illustration section.

A special thank you goes to our editors at Watson-Guptill: Executive Editor Mary Suffudy and Senior Editor Candace Raney, for their enthusiasm and encouragement, and Associate Editor Paul Lukas, for his expertise and understanding.

Special thanks are also due to John Pfeufer, who designed many of the assignment sheets, along with Jean Cronin, Thomas Gianfagna, Meryl L. Meyer, and Elizabeth Rosenthal. The art throughout the book was diligently photograhed by Maurice Sherman.

Finally, this endeavor would not have been possible without the assistance of the Visual Arts Press, Ltd., which printed the original assignment sheets that are reproduced in the book.

The following assignments address the complex issue of graphic design instruction. Each assignment, or *problem,* is carefully structured to create conditions conducive to discovering the language of graphic design. These conditions encourage exploration of visual communication concepts and design principles, allowing students to develop more personally expressive ways of solving communication problems.

Under this instructive approach, personal, intuitive concepts are stressed over specific technical skills. These skills and techniques needed to execute the assignments are not taught; they must be *developed,* through involvement with the problems. This interactive approach is ideally suited to the world of graphic design—a world of dynamic concepts and ever-changing ideas.

BLACK SQUARE PROBLEM: By using four black squares of the same dimension, create a graphic image that best expresses the meaning of each of the following six words (see below). Make eight preliminary sketches for each word in the areas indicated. Then select the most effective solution and execute it in the larger designated area. Using only four squares is a seemingly limited palette to express such diverse words, yet these squares can be expanded into a more comprehensive language by utilizing various design principles.

ORDER

INCREASE

BOLD

CONGESTED

TENSION

PLAYFUL

ORDER

INCREASE

BOLD

CONGESTED

TENSION

PLAYFUL

BLACK SQUARE PROBLEM:

By using four flat black squares of the same dimension, create a graphic image to express the meaning of each of the following six words: *order, increase, bold, congested, tension,* and *playful.* Make eight preliminary sketches for each word in the areas indicated. Then select the most effective solution for each and execute it in the larger designated area. Using only four squares may seem to be a rather limited palette for expressing such diverse words, but consider how these squares can be expanded into a more comprehensive language by utilizing various design principles.

Analysis: The intention of this problem is to develop a geometric idiom through the discovery of the various two-dimensional design principles needed to extend a limited graphic vocabulary. The necessary principles include: framal reference; touching; overlapping and cropping of forms; illusory space; contrast of elements in terms of size, direction, space, and position; and the dynamics of negative–positive relationships.

The discoveries result from experimentation with the interrelationships of forms, a vital experience for the growth of a designer developing a personal, formal style. Combining these principles can further expand a mere graphic vocabulary into a comprehensive, abstract graphic language, maximizing the possibilities for graphic expression.

Notes: Because design skills become more comprehensive by creating several solutions for a single problem, selecting the *most effective* solution is an important condition explored through this assignment.

Through the use of perspective, the four squares can be of differing sizes, furthering the range of possible solutions. Many students use just this approach in their solutions, as can be seen on the following pages.

BLACK SQUARE SOLUTIONS:

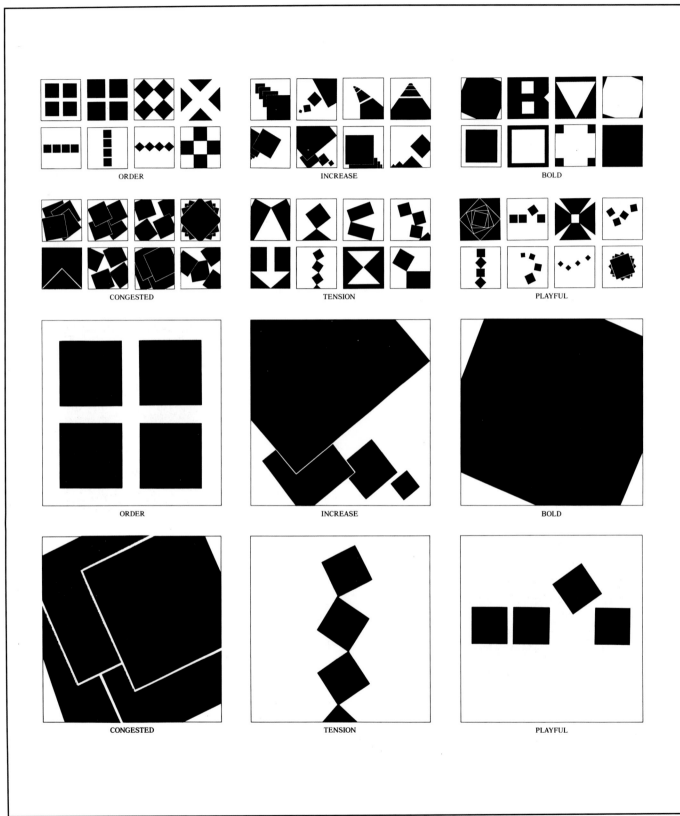

ORDER

INCREASE

BOLD

CONGESTED

TENSION

PLAYFUL

ORDER

INCREASE

BOLD

CONGESTED

TENSION

PLAYFUL

KOBY CAULY

18

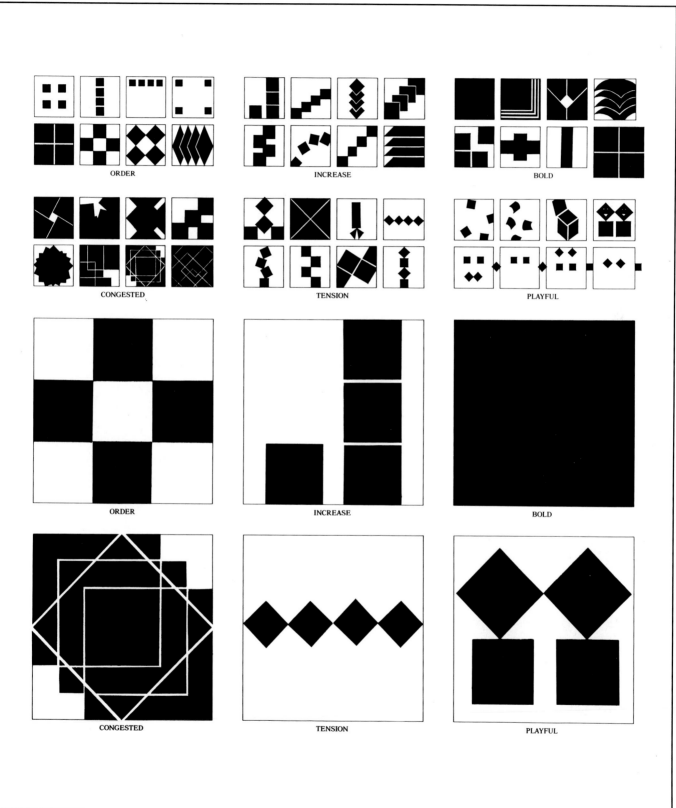

ORDER

INCREASE

BOLD

CONGESTED

TENSION

PLAYFUL

ORDER

INCREASE

BOLD

CONGESTED

TENSION

PLAYFUL

BLACK SQUARE SOLUTIONS:

1. CARIN POMBO
2. TRACY WETSTEIN
3. PEGGY DENOMME

1

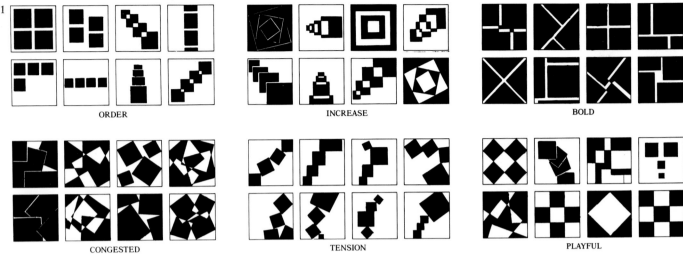

ORDER   INCREASE   BOLD

CONGESTED   TENSION   PLAYFUL

2

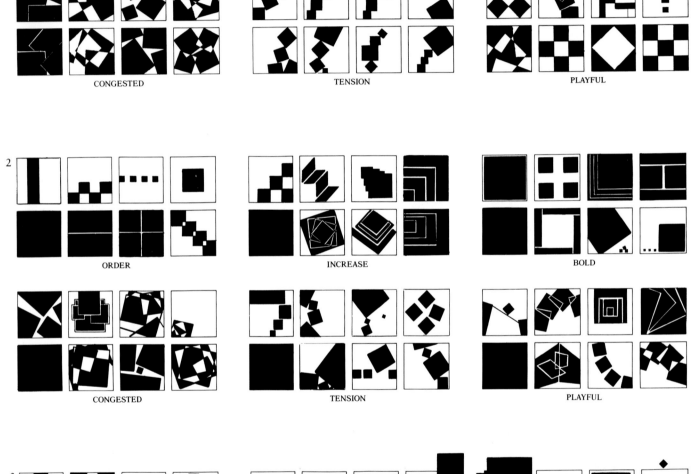

ORDER   INCREASE   BOLD

CONGESTED   TENSION   PLAYFUL

3

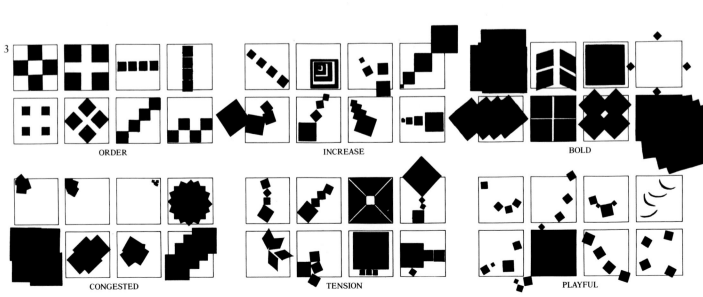

ORDER   INCREASE   BOLD

CONGESTED   TENSION   PLAYFUL

20

4. SOFIA PAIVA RAPOSO
5. NOEMI AYUSO
6. STEPHANIE ARCULLI

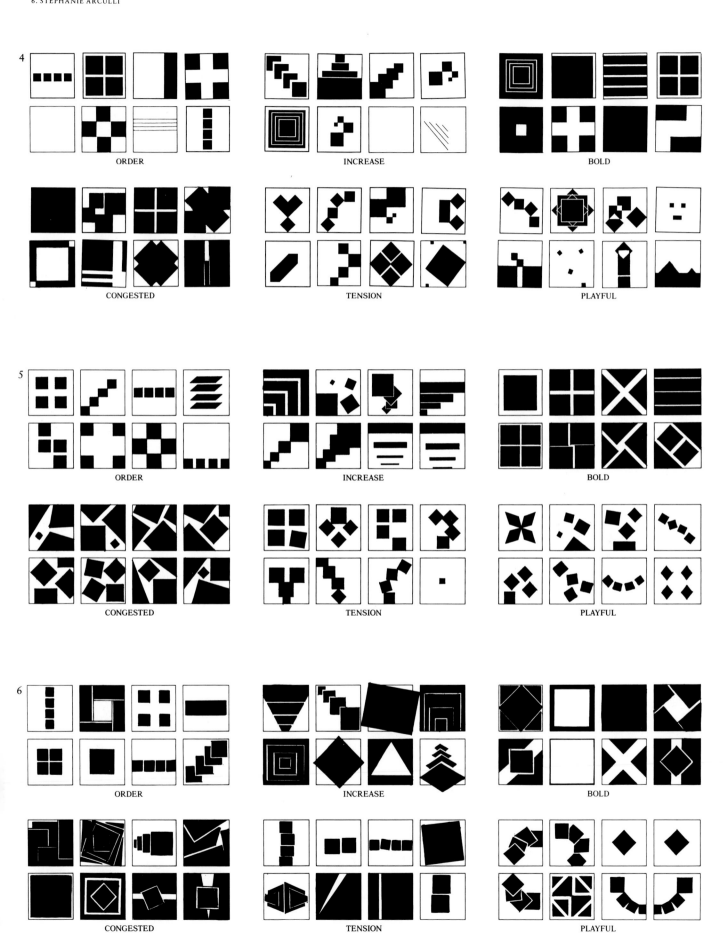

4

ORDER INCREASE BOLD

CONGESTED TENSION PLAYFUL

5

ORDER INCREASE BOLD

CONGESTED TENSION PLAYFUL

6

ORDER INCREASE BOLD

CONGESTED TENSION PLAYFUL

BLACK SQUARE SOLUTIONS:

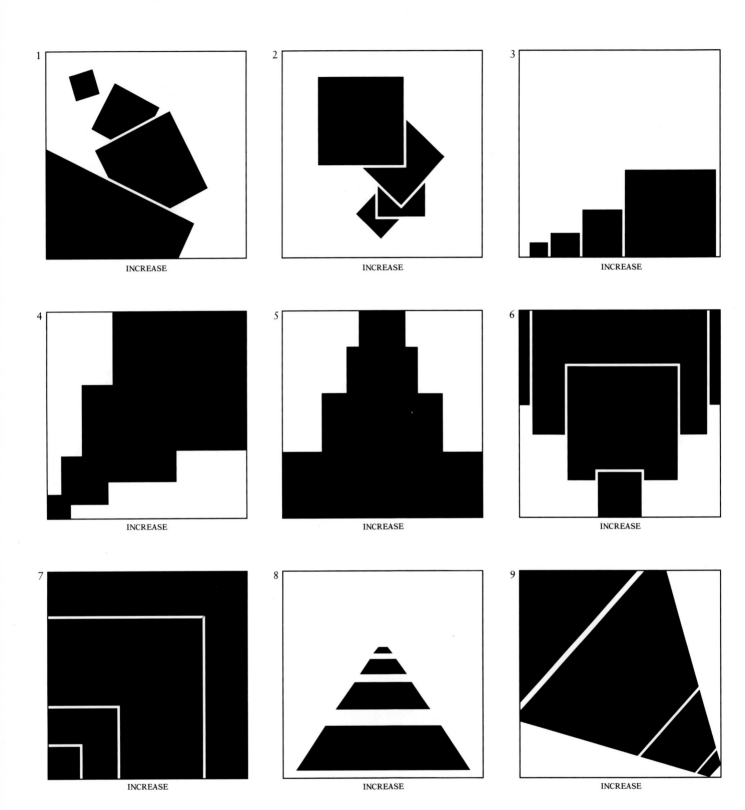

1
INCREASE

2
INCREASE

3
INCREASE

4
INCREASE

5
INCREASE

6
INCREASE

7
INCREASE

8
INCREASE

9
INCREASE

1. SANTINO FONTANA
2. NOEMI AYUSO
3. ELISA SANDONATO-ROBBINS
4. PARK MOON SUNG
5. DANIELA BARCELÓ
6. REBECCA RESTREPO

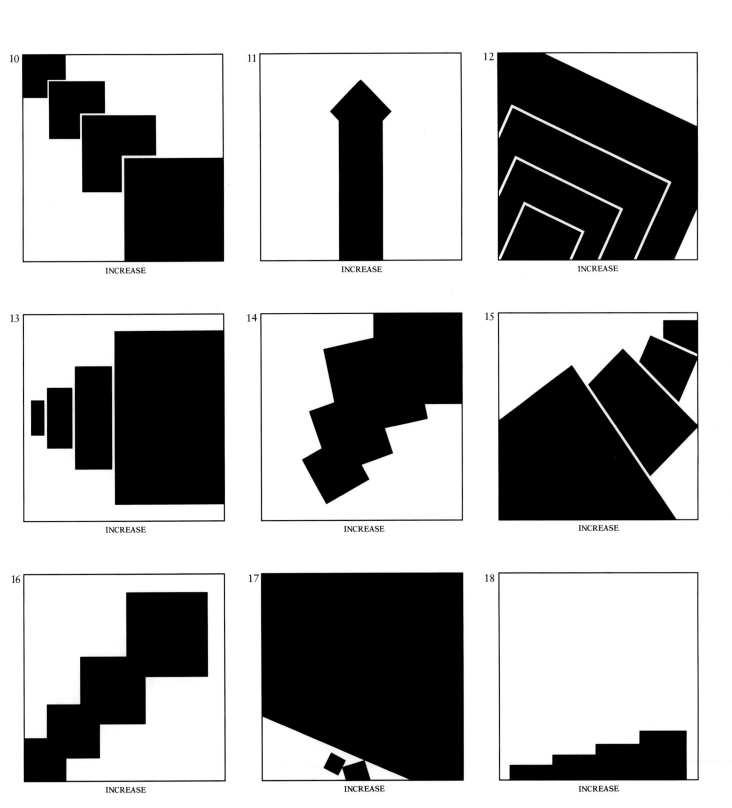

10 INCREASE

11 INCREASE

12 INCREASE

13 INCREASE

14 INCREASE

15 INCREASE

16 INCREASE

17 INCREASE

18 INCREASE

7. YU-ZHOU LUO
8. ELLEN SANTOS
9. JILLIAN MYERS
10. STEPHANIE ARCULLI
11. ANGELA PFEUFER
12. TEDD NELSON

13. ALEKSANDR PUCHLIK
14. ADAM SYMONS
15. SHARON HAREL
16. SOFIA PAIVA RAPOSO
17. JULIAN PEPLOE
18. PAGE EDWARDS

BLACK SQUARE SOLUTIONS:

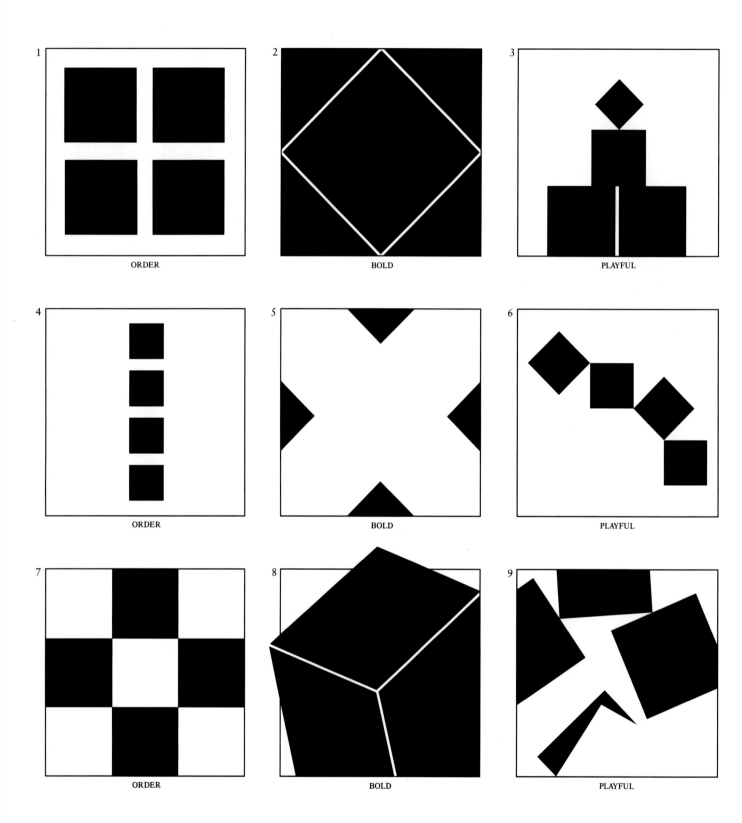

1 ORDER

2 BOLD

3 PLAYFUL

4 ORDER

5 BOLD

6 PLAYFUL

7 ORDER

8 BOLD

9 PLAYFUL

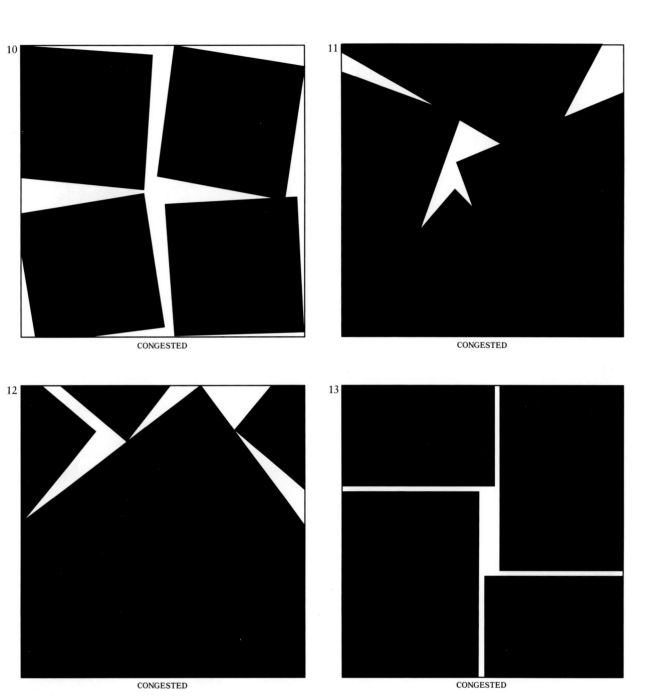

10

CONGESTED

11

CONGESTED

12

CONGESTED

13

CONGESTED

BLACK SQUARE SOLUTIONS:

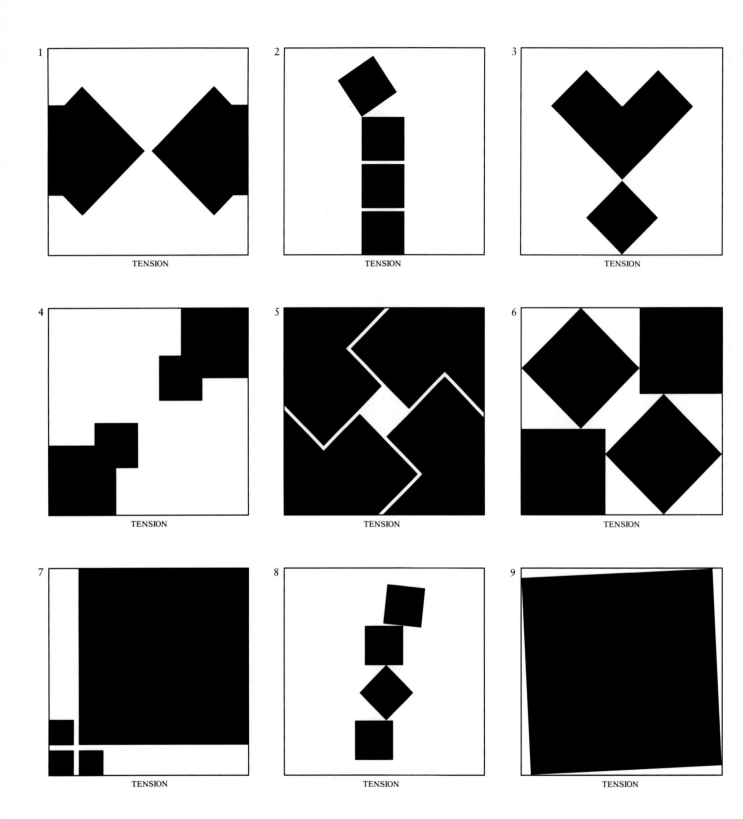

1   TENSION

2   TENSION

3   TENSION

4   TENSION

5   TENSION

6   TENSION

7   TENSION

8   TENSION

9   TENSION

26

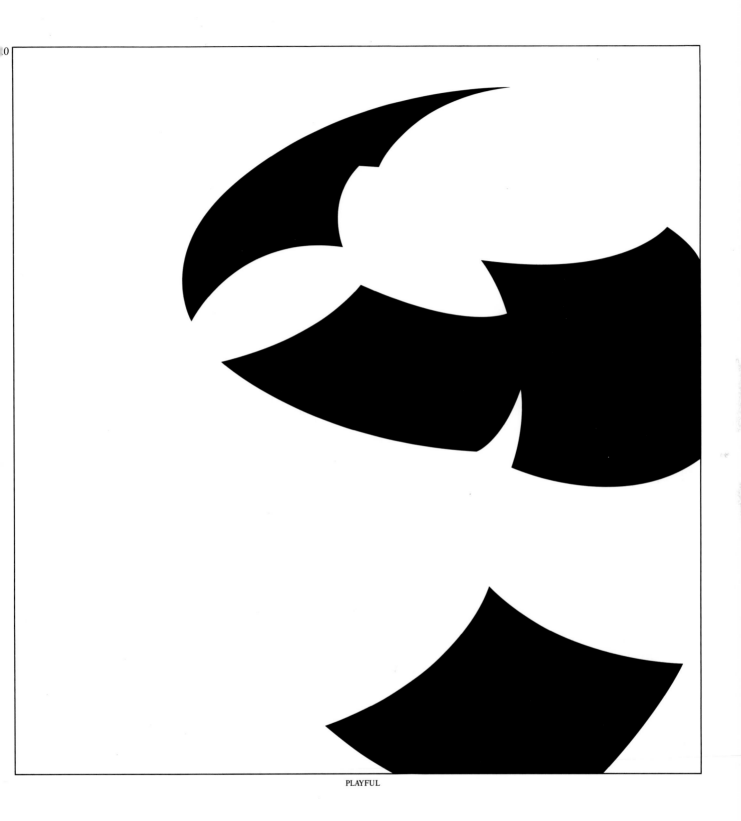

PLAYFUL

1. YUN-KYUNG BANG
2. SILVIA CESAR RIBEIRO
3. SOFIA PAIVA RAPOSO
4. YU-ZHOU LUO
5. JIMMY LUI
6. ALEKSANDR PUCHLIK
7. REBECCA RESTREPO
8. CARLOS BELTRÁN
9. STEPHANIE ARCULLI
10. PHILIP MC COBB

B L A C K

W H I T E

Negative space is an important aspect of graphic design. An equivalent of this is the Zen idea that the essence of a bowl is the part that is missing. Apply this idea to the graphic technique of using only negative shapes and visualize three of the following subjects: salt, ghost, cloud(s), whipped cream, Moby Dick, Jaws, sugar, polar bear, flour, smoke, vanilla ice-cream cone, and steam. The actual subjects themselves should not be drawn. Only the negative space can make for visually intriguing solutions. As a design consideration, the chosen images may be cropped. Use the smaller areas indicated for preliminary drawings and the larger areas for final executions.

1   2   3

BLACK AND WHITE PROBLEM:

The Zen concept that a bowl's essence is the part that is "missing" corresponds to the graphic concept of negative space. Apply this idea by using only negative shapes to interpret three of the following subjects visually: clouds, whipped cream, *Moby Dick*, *Jaws*, sugar, ghost, salt, polar bear, flour, smoke, vanilla ice-cream cone, and steam. The subjects themselves should not be drawn; only the surrounding negative space and possibly areas in shadow should be addressed, and only in the color black. As a design consideration, the images may be cropped to show only a portion of the subjects. Use the smaller areas for preliminary drawings and the larger areas for final executions.

Analysis: The idea of formulating an image by only addressing its background changes the habitual approach toward seeing. When viewers are led to focus solely on background and shadowed areas, it is the unmarked portion of the page—the white ground—that becomes magically transformed into a recognizable subject. The traditional image-making process is thereby reversed, with a greater emphasis on compositional concerns, negative–positive relationships, and framal reference.

These images tend to encourage viewers to reverse the images' negative and positive fields mentally, making the positive areas become negative and vice versa. The classic goblet–profiles image is a good example of this.

The study of volume and light is another area of exploration within this problem. Through the subtle articulation of light and shadow, an entire image can be implied. This allows the viewer to participate by instinctively completing the missing visual information, thereby becoming directly involved with the piece. This mechanism, like the concept of negative and positive forms reversing themselves, challenges the viewer's attention—which is the goal of visual communication.

Note: To clarify the meaning of what negative and positive relationships are, it should be understood that images appearing on the *page surface* are positive, while anything appearing farther back in space is negative. Black does not necessarily represent the negative space.

B L A C K

W H I T E

Negative space is an important aspect of graphic design. An equivalent of this is the Zen idea that the essence of a bowl is the part that is missing. Apply this idea to the graphic technique of using only negative shapes and visualize three (3) of the following subjects: cloud(s), whipped cream, Moby Dick, Jaws, sugar, ghost, salt, polar bear, flour, smoke, vanilla ice cream cone and steam. The actual subjects themselves should not be drawn. Only the negative space can make for visually intriguing solutions. As a design consideration, the chosen images may be cropped. Use the smaller areas indicated for preliminary drawings and the larger areas for final executions.

1   2   3

CARIN POMBO

ALEKSANDR PUCHLIK

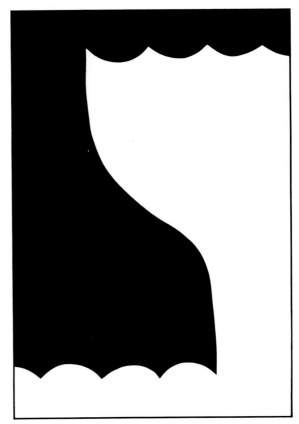

KOBY CAULY

STEPHEN CANNATO

ALEKSANDR PUCHLIK

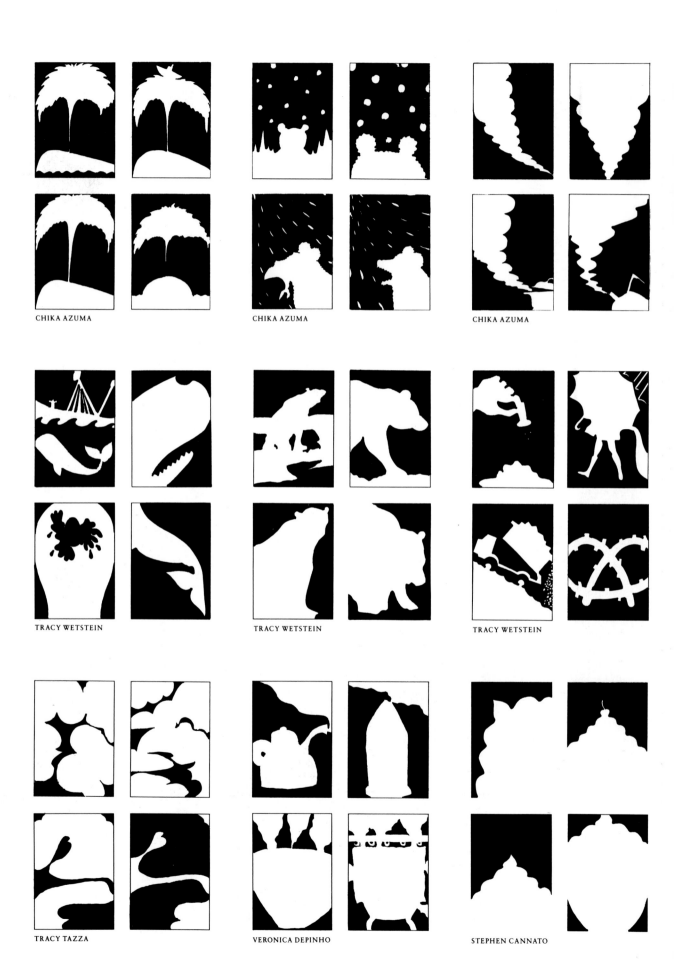

CHIKA AZUMA

CHIKA AZUMA

CHIKA AZUMA

TRACY WETSTEIN

TRACY WETSTEIN

TRACY WETSTEIN

TRACY TAZZA

VERONICA DEPINHO

STEPHEN CANNATO

CHIKA AZUMA

BLACK AND WHITE SOLUTIONS:

FRANK CASTALDI

FRANK CASTALDI

SHARON HAREL

PEGGY DENOMME

CHANG MIN HAN

CHIKA AZUMA

TRACY WETSTEIN

REBECCA RESTREPO

CHIKA AZUMA

LEAH CAPLAN

PEGGY DENOMME

TOHRU KANAYAMA

TRACY WETSTEIN

VERONICA DEPINHO

VERONICA DEPINHO

PEGGY DENOMME

REBECCA RESTREPO

TRACY TAZZA

SOO-JEOUNG KIM

REBECCA RESTREPO

GARY TAM

BLACK AND WHITE SOLUTIONS:

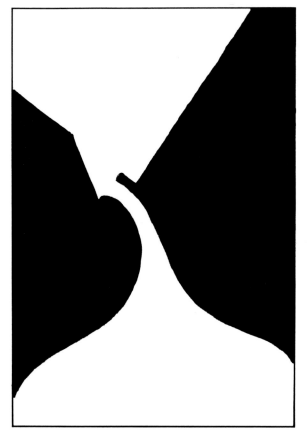

JILLIAN MYERS

ADAM SYMONS

DAPHNE WIEDLING

JOANNE GONZALEZ

IP KWOK PO BOCO

JIMMY LUI

SOFIA PAIVA RAPOSO

Selecting a successful solution from a large number of choices is in itself a very important aspect of the design process, and consequently appears in many of the assignments throughout this book. Editing—especially *self*-editing—is a critical skill that requires an inner sense or understanding of what attracts one's own attention (the most obvious barometer for assessing impacts on viewers' attentions) while keeping in mind the precise intent of the problem. Good editing skills reinforce good problem-solving skills, and vice versa.

JACK & JILL

P R O B L E M

In the six areas indicated, create visual equivalents to best express each part of the nursery rhyme ''Jack and Jill'' by using the dingbats and/or punctuation marks below. These symbols can be used individually or combined to develop a personal visual metaphor. When executing your solutions, use a photocopier, stat camera, or lucigraph to enlarge the selected graphic images to the appropriate size of the given space. Use either black and white or color.

JACK AND JILL

WENT UP THE HILL

TO FETCH A PAIL OF WATER

JACK FELL DOWN

AND BROKE HIS CROWN

AND JILL CAME TUMBLING AFTER.

P R O B L E M S : S O L U T I O N S   S E R I E S

40

JACK AND JILL PROBLEM:

In the six areas indicated, create visual equivalents for each part of the nursery rhyme "Jack and Jill" by using the dingbats and/or punctuation marks given on the assignment sheet. These marks, symbols, and pictograms can be used individually or combined to develop a visual metaphor. Execute your solutions in black and white, unless your concept dictates otherwise.

Analysis: The intent of the Jack and Jill Problem is to develop a visual vocabulary within the parameters of a given set of images, allowing an opportunity to discover and grapple with the infinite possibilities that exist in what might first be perceived as a limited language. This assignment also presents a chance to respond freely to a timeworn nursery rhyme, taking something familiar and revitalizing it through the manipulation of images. This approach expands a designer's problem-solving vocabulary.

Along with other formal ideas, this problem encompasses illusory space, the dynamics of composition and scale relative to the given framal reference, and the cropping, intersecting, and overlapping of images. A primary concern here is the investigation of negative–positive relationships, which distinguish an image's surface design from its illusory space. The movement from the picture plane to illusory space and vice versa, if articulated with sensitivity, can have considerable power to attract and hold the viewer's attention.

Notes: The "Jack and Jill" nursery rhyme describes a period of time supported by a sequential visual theme. The movement from one frame to the next is an important design consideration to be addressed.

If possible, a photocopier that can shoot at different percentages should be used to enlarge or reduce the chosen images to the appropriate sizes relative to the work areas.

JACK & JILL
P R O B L E M

In the six areas indicated, create visual equivalents to best express each part of the nursery rhyme "Jack and Jill" by using the below ding bats and/or punctuation marks. These symbols can be used individually or combined to develop a personal visual metaphor. When executing your solutions, use a photocopier, stat camera or lucigraph to enlarge the selected graphic images to the appropriate size of the given space. Use either black and white or color.

JACK AND JILL

WENT UP THE HILL

TO FETCH A PAIL OF WATER

JACK FELL DOWN

AND BROKE HIS CROWN

AND JILL CAME TUMBLING AFTER.

P R O B L E M S : S O L U T I O N S S E R I E S

LISA MAZUR

Moving from a literal posture to a deeper understanding of a problem can give rise to the symbolic language of the visual metaphor. Such a development is the intention of this problem.

It is easy to be taken by the nursery rhyme's narrative, missing the real intent of the problem. This tendency is reinforced by reflexive literal conceptualization, which often results in predictable, unimaginative solutions. This superficial understanding must be transcended to create more meaningful graphic statements.

LISA MAZUR

AND JILL CAME TUMBLING AFTER

JACK AND JILL SOLUTIONS:

1. TRACY WETSTEIN
2. MOON SUNG PARK
3. IP KWOK PO BOCO
4. I-HSUAN WANG

1

JACK AND JILL

WENT UP THE HILL

TO FETCH A PAIL OF WATER

JACK FELL DOWN

AND BROKE HIS CROWN

AND JILL CAME TUMBLING AFTER.

2

JACK AND JILL

WENT UP THE HILL

TO FETCH A PAIL OF WATER

JACK FELL DOWN

AND BROKE HIS CROWN

AND JILL CAME TUMBLING AFTER.

44

3

JACK AND JILL

WENT UP THE HILL

TO FETCH A PAIL OF WATER

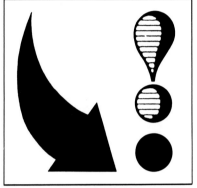

JACK FELL DOWN

AND BROKE HIS CROWN

AND JILL CAME TUMBLING AFTER.

4

JACK AND JILL

WENT UP THE HILL

TO FETCH A PAIL OF WATER

JACK FELL DOWN

AND BROKE HIS CROWN

AND JILL CAME TUMBLING AFTER.

JACK AND JILL SOLUTIONS:

1

TO FETCH A PAIL OF WATER

2

WENT UP THE HILL

3

WENT UP THE HILL

4

WENT UP THE HILL

5

JACK AND JILL

6

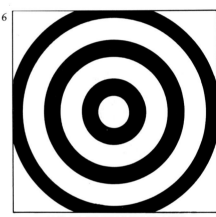

AND JILL CAME TUMBLING AFTER.

7

TO FETCH A PAIL OF WATER

8

JACK FELL DOWN

9

AND BROKE HIS CROWN

1. ANN MATHIS
2. JIMMY LUI
3. STEPHANIE ARCULLI
4. CHRIS SOCCIO
5. KLAUS GANER JOHANSEN
6. KOBY CAULY

WENT UP THE HILL

JACK FELL DOWN

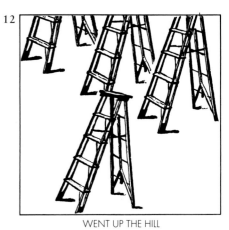

WENT UP THE HILL

TO FETCH A PAIL OF WATER

JACK FELL DOWN

AND BROKE HIS CROWN

WENT UP THE HILL

JACK FELL DOWN

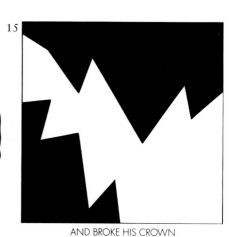

TO FETCH A PAIL OF WATER

JACK AND JILL SOLUTIONS:

1. I. RODRIGUEZ
2. EILEEN CARROLL
3. SOFIA PAIVA RAPOSO
4. MIN-HUI CHANG

1

JACK AND JILL

WENT UP THE HILL

TO FETCH A PAIL OF WATER

JACK FELL DOWN

AND BROKE HIS CROWN

AND JILL CAME TUMBLING AFTER.

2

JACK AND JILL

WENT UP THE HILL

TO FETCH A PAIL OF WATER

JACK FELL DOWN

AND BROKE HIS CROWN

AND JILL CAME TUMBLING AFTER.

3

JACK AND JILL

WENT UP THE HILL

TO FETCH A PAIL OF WATER

JACK FELL DOWN

AND BROKE HIS CROWN

AND JILL CAME TUMBLING AFTER.

4

JACK AND JILL

WENT UP THE HILL

TO FETCH A PAIL OF WATER

JACK FELL DOWN

AND BROKE HIS CROWN

AND JILL CAME TUMBLING AFTER.

JACK AND JILL SOLUTIONS:

1

JACK AND JILL

WENT UP THE HILL

TO FETCH A PAIL OF WATER

JACK FELL DOWN

AND BROKE HIS CROWN

AND JILL CAME TUMBLING AFTER.

JACK AND JILL

WENT UP THE HILL

The question at hand for the Jack and Jill Problem is how to take the given problem and change it, reinterpret it, redefine it, and restate it, so that it carries personal significance. This activity of making a problem personally interesting has great importance: Not only is there the possibility of attracting others through unique solutions, but this is where artists can address inner needs by resolving their own aesthetic sensibilities. This gives tangibility and meaning to the personal design process, and it is in this act that real growth begins, ultimately leading to the delicate balance between inner growth and communicative problem solving.

1. SYLVIA FINZI
2. ERIC C. KING

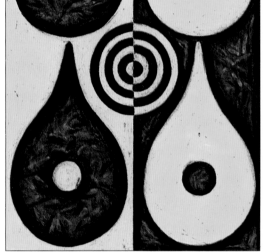

TO FETCH A PAIL OF WATER

JACK FELL DOWN

AND BROKE HIS CROWN

AND JILL CAME TUMBLING AFTER.

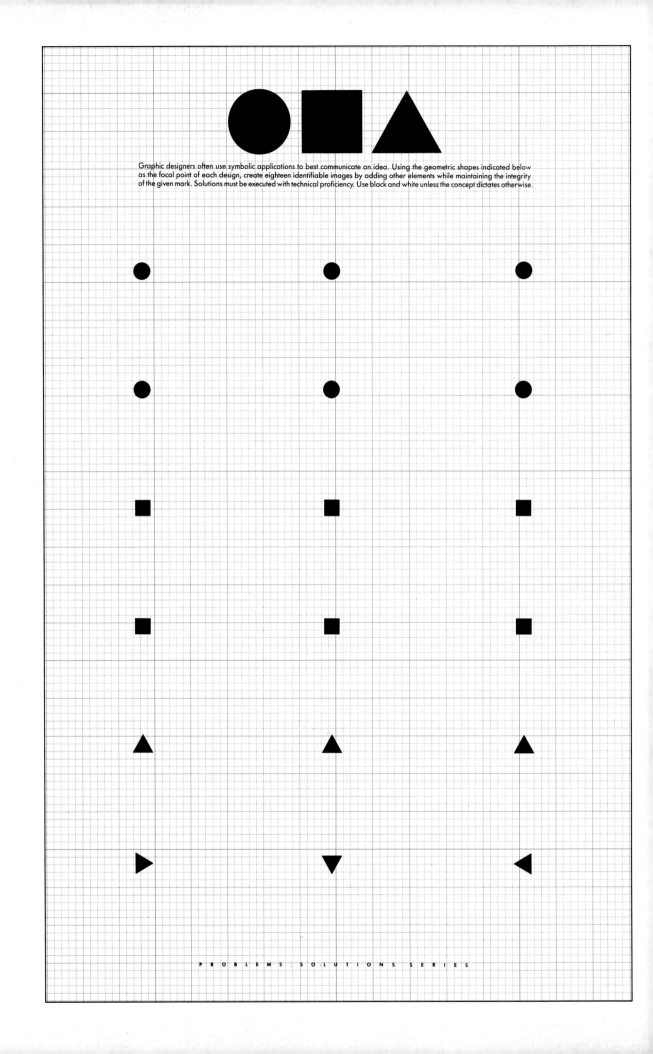

Graphic designers often use symbolic applications to best communicate an idea. Using the geometric shapes indicated below as the focal point of each design, create eighteen identifiable images by adding other elements while maintaining the integrity of the given mark. Solutions must be executed with technical proficiency. Use black and white unless the concept dictates otherwise.

CIRCLE, SQUARE, TRIANGLE PROBLEM:

Graphic designers often use geometry to communicate an idea. Using the circles, squares, and triangles indicated on the assignment sheet as focal points, create eighteen identifiable images by adding other elements while maintaining the integrity of the original shapes. Solutions must be executed with technical proficiency in black and white, unless your concept dictates otherwise.

Analysis: Geometry, often used in the design of signage and corporate identity, introduces designers to the process of creating a reductive language for visual communication. It is possible to solve this problem by relying solely on mechanical methods, using drafting tools, templates, French curves, and so on. Under this approach, design sensibilities are called upon, while drawing skills take a secondary role.

Notes: Some designers may respond to the geometric images by creating complex illustrations in direct contrast to the elemental simplicity of the geometric forms. Although this is not the intent of the problem, it is nonetheless a valid personal image-making approach, demonstrating how most problems serve as gateways to the possibilities of graphic communications, sometimes at the expense of original intention.

Credits for the solutions appearing on pages 56 through 63 are listed on page 190.

CIRCLE, SQUARE, TRIANGLE SOLUTIONS:

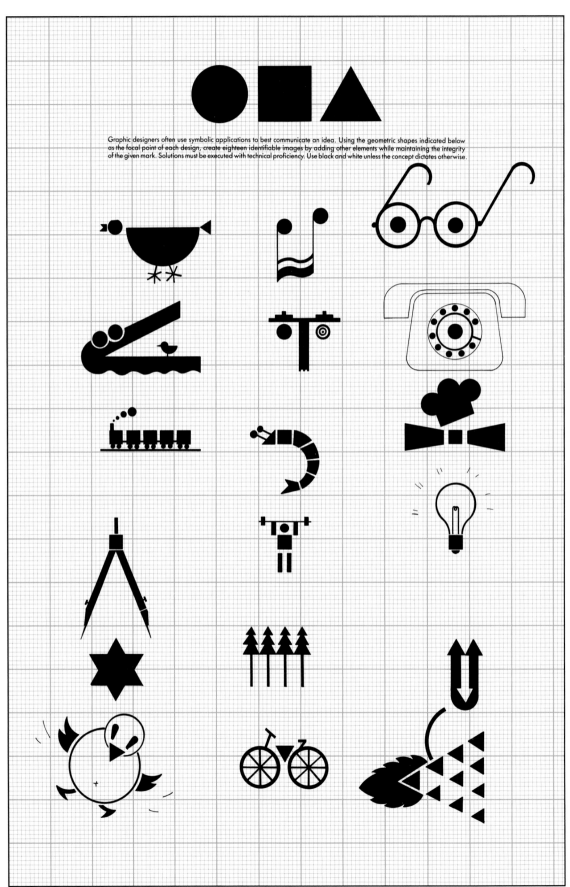

Graphic designers often use symbolic applications to best communicate an idea. Using the geometric shapes indicated below as the focal point of each design, create eighteen identifiable images by adding other elements while maintaining the integrity of the given mark. Solutions must be executed with technical proficiency. Use black and white unless the concept dictates otherwise.

YOUMI HEO

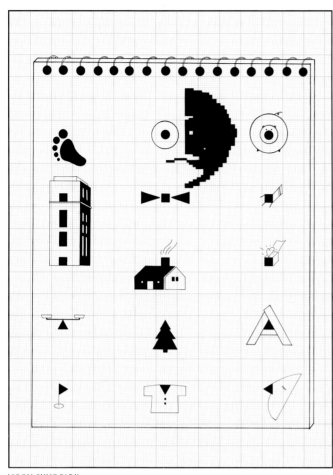

MOON-SUNG PARK

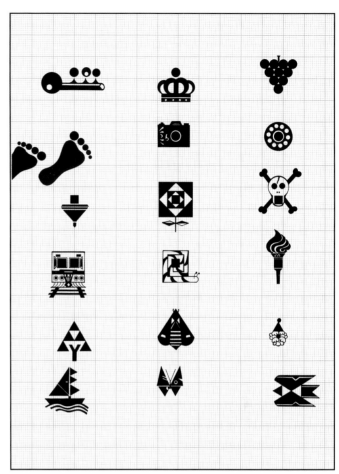

DANIELA BARCELÓ

CLAUDIA GNADINGER

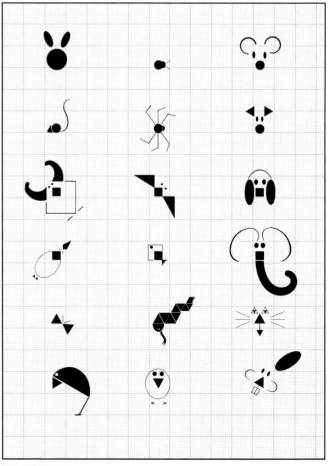

MIN-HUI CHANG

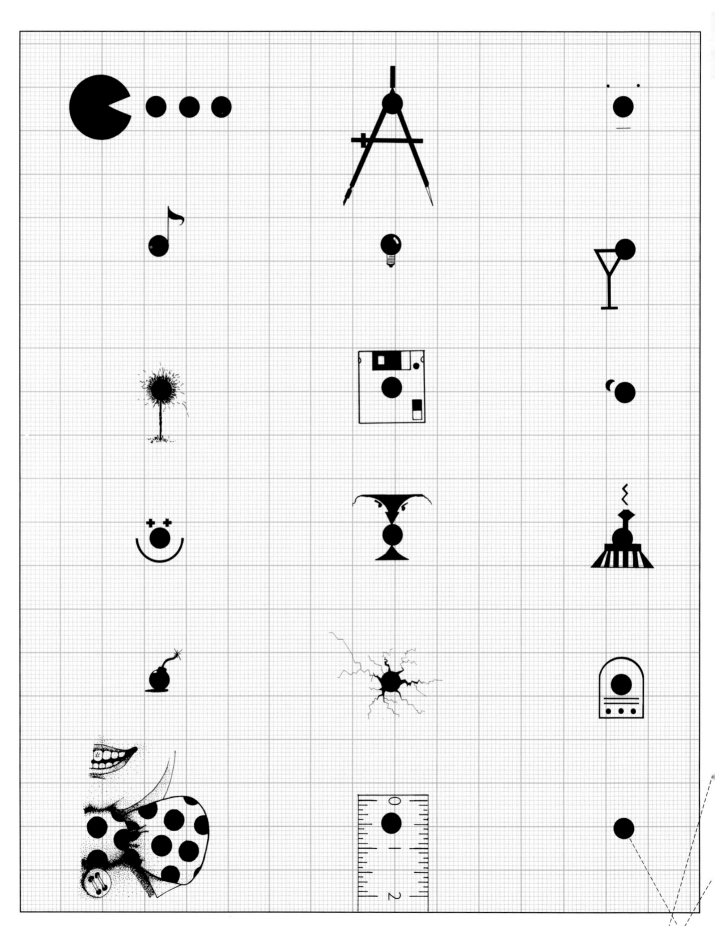

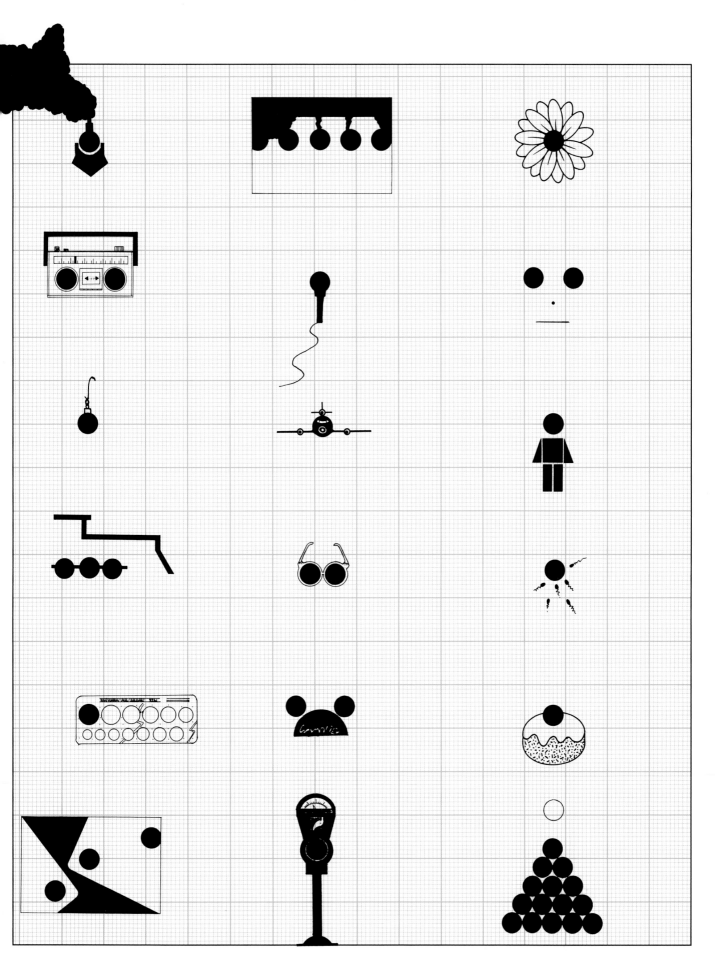

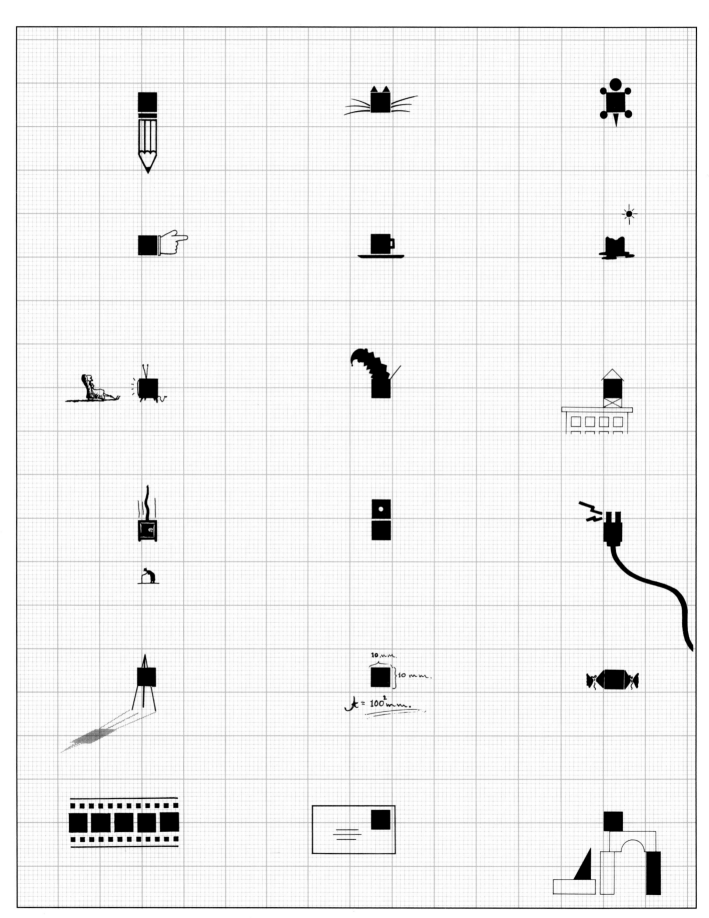

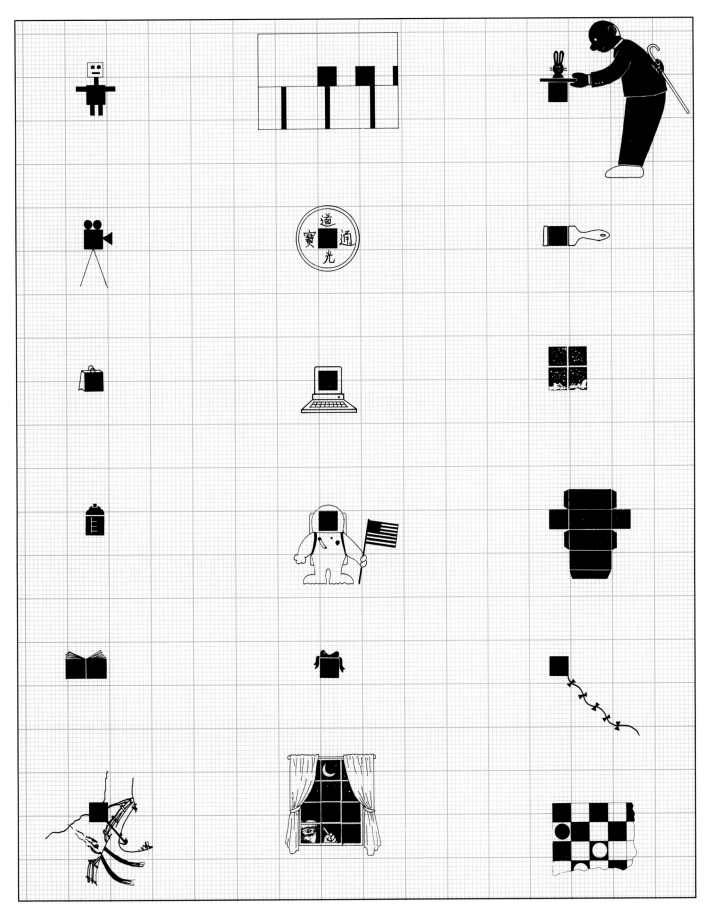

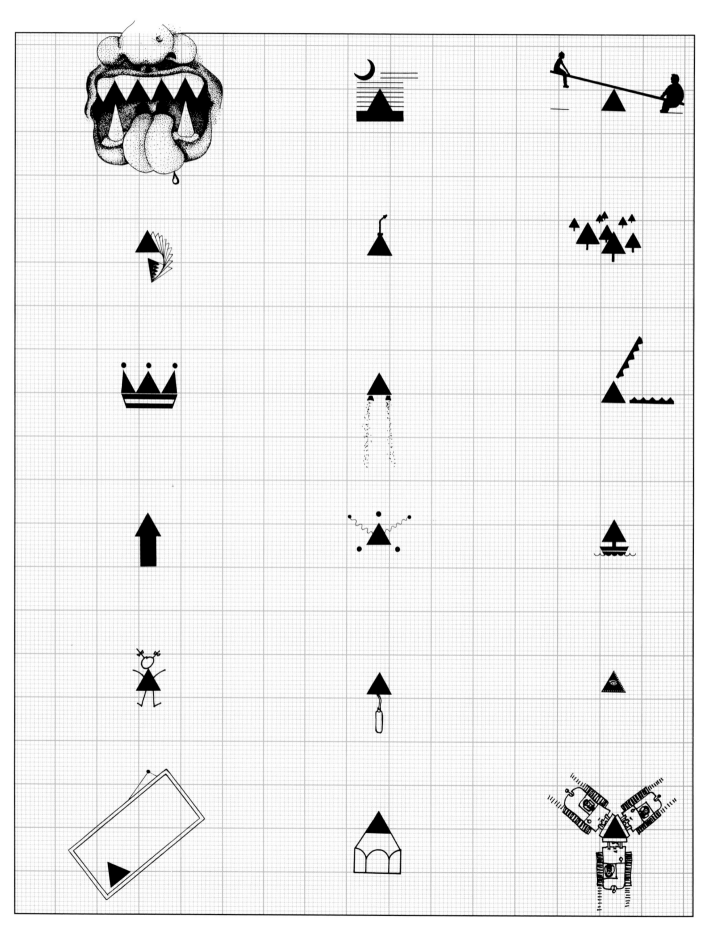

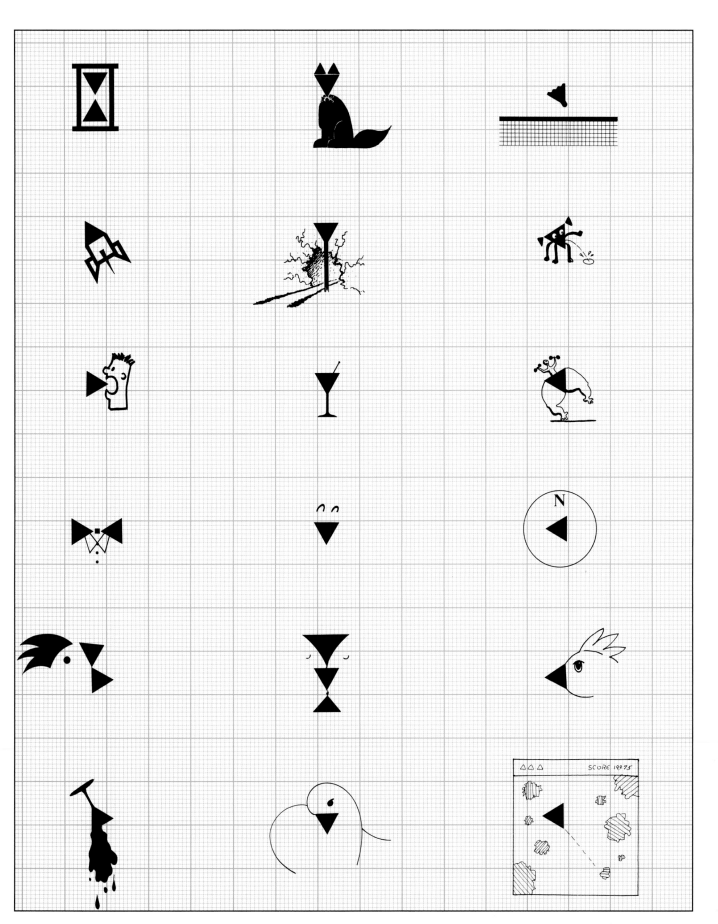

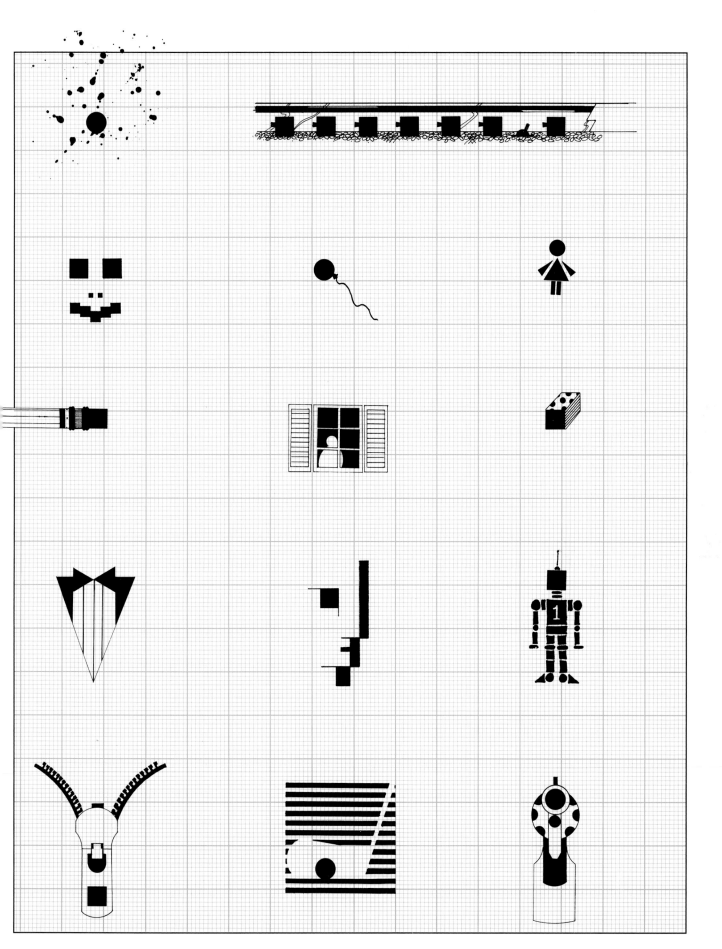

Mies van der Rohe (signature)

Suggesting an image is the graphic counterpart of Mies van der Rohe's idea that "less is more." This approach is a powerful technique that a graphic designer can employ in communicating an idea. It creates a situation where the viewing audience interacts with the artwork by mentally completing the implied image. With thousands of images each day demanding our consideration, this condition, "less is more," helps in capturing one's attention. In the areas below, solve the following six problems as indicated.

1   2   3

Problem #1. In keeping with the idea "less is more," choose one of the following: an industrial object, animal, plant, or insect, and using black and white only, design it in its entirety by simplifying its physical characteristics into flat negative and positive shapes.

Problem #2. Crop the original design you created for Problem #1, yet retain its readability.

Problem #3. Drastically crop the design you created for Problem #1 so readability is no longer a factor. Abstract shapes are the main concern.

Choose one of the 3 previously created designs (either solution #1, 2, or 3) and execute this same image in the next three areas as instructed.

Problem #4. Reverse the chosen design in its entirety. All black areas become white while all white areas become black. This holds true for the background as well.

Problem #5. Execute the chosen design using black and white plus one additional color.

Problem #6. Execute the chosen design in full color.

4   5   6

Suggesting an image, rather than directly depicting it, is the graphic counterpart of Mies van der Rohe's idea, *less is more.* This reductive approach is a powerful technique that a graphic designer can employ, inviting the viewing audience to interact with the artwork by mentally completing the implied image. This problem is a six-part assignment taking the designer through various stages useful in creating such an image. The six parts of the problem are to be executed as follows:

1. In keeping with the less-is-more idea, choose an industrial object, animal, or plant, and, using black and white only, design it in its entirety by simplifying its physical characteristics into flat negative and positive shapes.

2. Crop the original design you created for step 1, but retain its readability.

3. Drastically crop the design you created for step 1, to the point where recognizability is no longer a factor—abstract shapes are the main concern.

4. Choosing one of the designs from steps 1, 2, or 3, execute the chosen design in reverse-field—all black areas become white, all white areas become black, for both subject and background.

5. Execute the chosen design using black and white plus one additional color.

6. Execute the chosen design in full color.

Analysis: Creating a simple black-and-white graphic image is a complex design procedure that is fertile ground for experimentation. However, the primary intention of this problem is to move past this point and introduce other design options, which are created by altering the initial design and lie in the realm of the reductive approach.

In step 1, images appear farther back in space, which gives the feeling of a more traditional composition. A tightly cropped image (step 2) puts much of the visual information on the surface of the page, giving it a graphic quality by calling close attention to its negative and positive relationships; a severely cropped image (step 3) moves into the realm of abstraction, where the language of the image centers on form. Designers must be very sensitive to the cropping of an image, because various croppings connote different meanings. A seemingly subtle alteration can drastically affect the nature of an image. In steps 4, 5, and 6, the image is altered further: Reversing an image (step 4) can give rise to a new vision; the addition of one or more colors (steps 5 and 6), although additive in nature, deals with simplified surface applications only, and therefore is not necessarily in conflict with the spirit of a reductive approach, maintaining the less-is-more concept and making the final solution an even more personal one.

Suggesting an image is the graphic counterpart of Mies van der Rohe's idea that "less is more." This approach is a powerful technique that a graphic designer can employ in communicating an idea. It creates a situation where the viewing audience interacts with the artwork by mentally completing the implied image. With thousands of images each day demanding our consideration, this condition, "less is more," helps in capturing one's attention. In the areas below, solve the following six problems as indicated.

LESS IS MORE

1   2   3

Problem #1. In keeping with the idea "Less is More", choose one of the following: an industrial object, animal, plant, or insect, and using black and white only, design it in its entirety by simplifying its physical characteristics into flat negative and positive shapes.

Problem #2. Crop the original design you created for Problem #1, yet retain its readability.

Problem #3. Drastically crop the design you created for Problem #1 so readability is no longer a factor. Abstract shapes are the main concern.

Choose one of the 3 previously created designs (either solution #1, 2, or 3) and execute this same image in the next three areas as instructed.

  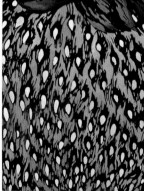

Problem #4. Reverse the chosen design in its entirety. All black areas become white while all white areas become black. This holds true for the background as well.

Problem #5. Execute the chosen design using black and white plus one additional color.

Problem #6. Execute the chosen design in full color.

4   5   6

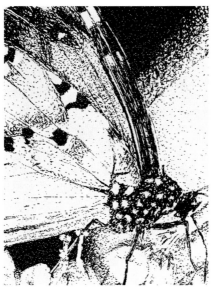

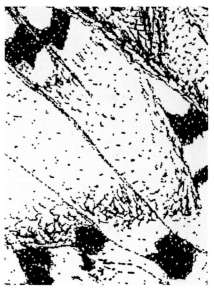

Problem #1. In keeping with the idea "less is more," choose one of the following: an industrial object, animal, plant, or insect, and using black and white only, design it in its entirety by simplifying its physical characteristics into flat negative and positive shapes.

Problem #2. Crop the original design you created for Problem #1, yet retain its readability.

Problem #3. Drastically crop the design you created for Problem #1 so readability is no longer a factor. Abstract shapes are the main concern.

Choose one of the 3 previously created designs (either solution #1, 2, or 3) and execute this same image in the next three areas as instructed.

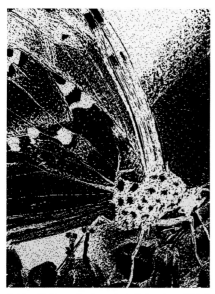

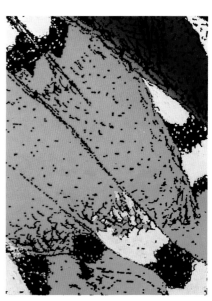

Problem #4. Reverse the chosen design in its entirety. All black areas become white while all white areas become black. This holds true for the background as well.

Problem #5. Execute the chosen design using black and white plus one additional color.

Problem #6. Execute the chosen design in full color.

Above:
ROSANA RAGUSA

Left:
LYNETTE MARIE ZATOR

YOUMI HEO

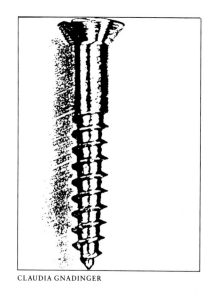
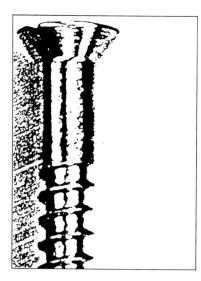

CLAUDIA GNADINGER

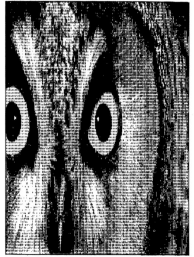
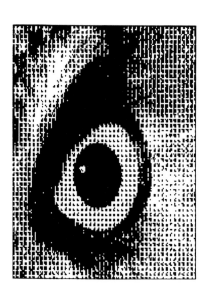
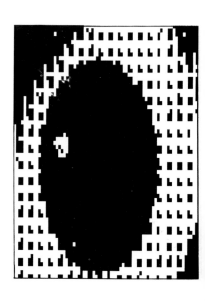

FRANK ASCONE

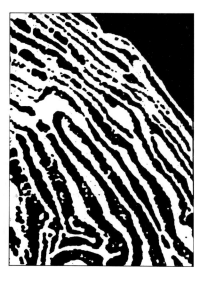  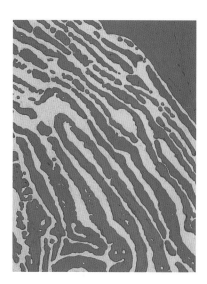

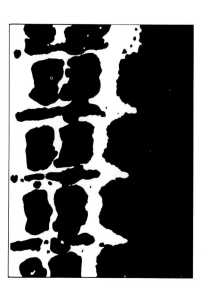 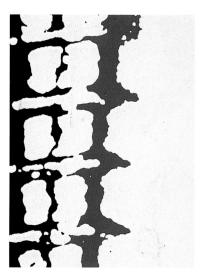 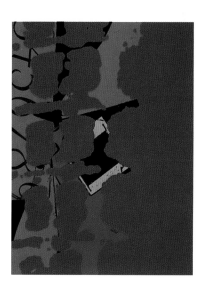

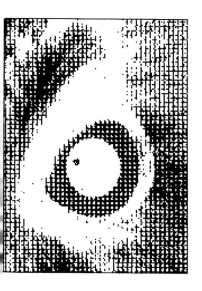  

LESS IS MORE SOLUTIONS:

JUNIOR VELOZ

PAUL VILLACIS

ROGER SCHINKLER

ROSANA RAGUSA

ROGER CAMP

IP KWOK PO BOCO

LESS IS MORE SOLUTIONS:

MIN-HUI CHANG

STEVE LAM

EVA MARIE PATURZO

The activity of cropping may seem obvious or be taken for granted, yet it is an important design consideration that is nurtured in this assignment.

FRANK CASTALDI

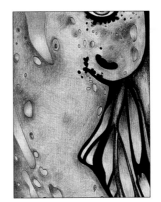

SYLVIA FINZI

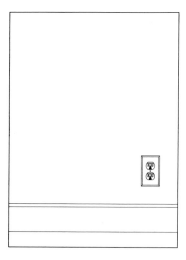

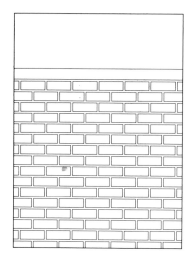

THE ALTERED PAGE

"The function of art is to defamiliarize the familiar." By altering, rearranging, changing, redesigning a commonplace image, one creates a new impression, which can capture the attention of one's audience. In an effort to accomplish this, redefine the three images above by altering them in a personal way. Execute each solution as accurately as possible by using black and white or full color.

ALTERED PAGE PROBLEM:

Altering, rearranging, changing, or redesigning a commonplace image can create a new impression to capture an audience's attention. With this in mind, each of the three images on the assignment sheet are to be redefined by altering them in a personal way. Solutions may range from literal storytelling to metaphoric imagery to abstractions, for this is a subjective assignment and most any theme, idea, or approach is valid. There is no "right" or "wrong," as long as the solution is genuinely and personally expressed.

The three individual problems are ends in themselves, although considering the whole page as a single unit is encouraged. The external portion of the assignment sheet (what lies outside of the three images) can be used. Manipulation of the outline typeface used for the problem name is permissible as well. Solutions should be executed as technically proficient finished pieces in black and white or full color.

Analysis: The three images convey cold, alienated messages, both individually and collectively—they are mechanically executed and lack any trace of human or even organic involvement. The intent is to bring about a more personal, human quality by manipulating the given images. In the broadest sense, the stated conditions of this problem provide an open opportunity to play, minimizing fears of failure.

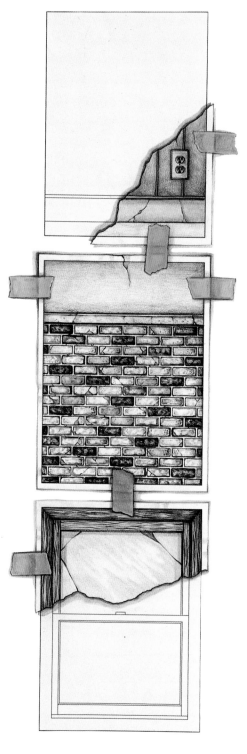

TARA PATTERSON

YOUMI HEO

BRIDGET HAWKINS

IP KWOK PO BOCO

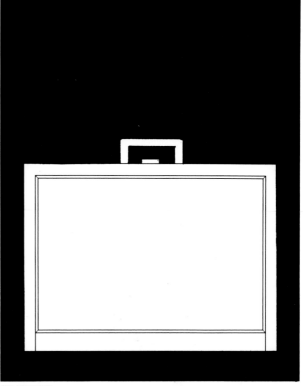

HSI-WEN LEE

ALTERED PAGE SOLUTIONS:

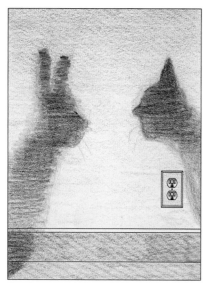

JESS M. PERNA

DAVID QUASHA

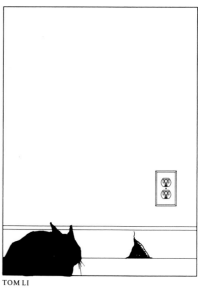

TOM LI

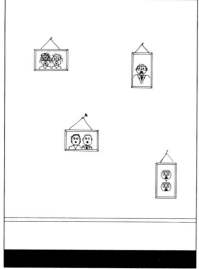

CATHERINE REBER

FRANK PELLEGRINO

CHENG-YI HSIAO

SHARON HAREL

IP KWOK PO BOCO

YOUMI HEO

STEPHEN CANNATO

CARMINDA SANTOS

STEPHEN CANNATO

CARMINDA SANTOS

ALTERED PAGE SOLUTIONS:

IP KWOK PO BOCO

TONY MONTES

FRANK PELLEGRINO

STEVEN LAM

JEFF SCHULZ

ROGER SCHICKLER

STEPHANIE ARCULLI

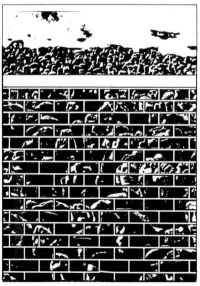

PAUL FISHER

YOUMI HEO

SANDRA LEISTER

REIKO IBUSUKI

WENDY SCHIMPF

PETER DELORENZO

BEVERLEY PERKIN

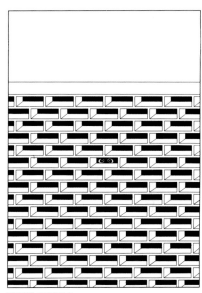

CHENG-YI HSIAO

MISSY WILLIAMS

BRIDGET HAWKINS

SHARON HAREL

The primary intentionof this problem is to explre various aspects of the fundamental design principle **contrast.** Students will experiment with negative/positive relationships, scale as it pertains to contrast, and patterning. Using only letterforms, create six typographic designs in the areas indicated creating typographic equivalents to solve the given problems. In each of the six problems use the designated typeface to simulate a printed piece. Use a minimum of two letterforms and as many colors as your concept dictates, except for the negative/positive problem, where only black and white is required. Note: Carefully consider the following design principles: framal reference, detachment, touching, overlapping, penetration, cropping, repetition, illusionary space, and contrast of shape, size, color, and direction.

Typeface: Caslon Bold, **Problem:** Scale

Typeface: Clarendon Bold, **Problem:** Negative/Positive

Typeface: Bodoni Bold, **Problem:** Pattern.

Typeface: Helvetica Extra Bold Condensed, **Problem:** Congestion

Typeface: Futura Black, **Problem:** Tension

Typeface: Ultra Bodoni, **Problem:** Playful

DESIGNING WITH TYPE PROBLEM:

Using only letterforms, create six typographic designs in the areas indicated on the assignment sheet. The essence of each design is to be created using only the designated typefaces. Use a minimum of two letterforms and as many colors as your concept dictates (except for the negative–positive problem, for which only black and white is required).

Analysis: All six problems are formalistic exercises in seeing letterforms' infinite possibilities as communication vehicles. The primary intention here is to explore various aspects of the fundamental design principle of *contrast*. Negative–positive relationships, scale, and patterning are explored. By experimenting with type within the parameters of these design principles, designers can develop basic skills into personal expressive repertoires.

Note: This problem is an extension of the Black Square Problem (see page 16). The major difference is that letterforms are substituted here for the black squares, and color now can play an important role.

DESIGNING WITH TYPE SOLUTIONS:

The primary intention of this problem is to explre various aspects of the fundamental design principle **contrast.** Students will experiment with negative/positive relationships, scale as it pertains to contrast, and patterning. Using only letterforms, create six typographic designs in the areas indicated creating typographic equivalents to solve the given problems. In each of the six problems use the designated typeface to simulate a printed piece. Use a minimum of two letterforms and as many colors as your concept dictates, except for the negative/positive problem, where only black and white is required. Note: Carefully consider the following design principles: framal reference, detachment, touching, overlapping, penetration, cropping, repetition, illusionary space, and contrast of shape, size, color, and direction.

Typeface: Caslon Bold, **Problem:** Scale

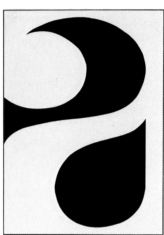

Typeface: Clarendon Bold, **Problem:** Negative/Positive

Typeface: Bodoni Bold, **Problem:** Pattern

Typeface: Helvetica Extra Bold Condensed, **Problem:** Congestion

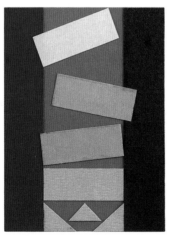

Typeface: Futura Black, **Problem:** Tension

Typeface: Ultra Bodoni, **Problem:** Playful

These twelve solutions address the issue of negative–positive relationships using Clarendon Bold. This problem represents a direct way of studying compositional aspects on a two-dimensional surface.

1. KOBY CAULY
2. LISA MAZUR
3. COSTANZA PUGLISI
4. MISSY WILLIAMS
5. BIRGITTE FJORD
6. KINDRA LOVEJOY
7. ROGER CAMP
8. FRANK ASCONE
9. ELISABETTA BERARDI
10. WENDY REITZEL
11. SYLVIA FINZI
12. YOUMI HEO

1

Typeface: Clarendon Bold, **Problem:** Negative/Positive

2

Typeface: Clarendon Bold, **Problem:** Negative/Positive

3

Typeface: Clarendon Bold, **Problem:** Negative/Positive

4

Typeface: Clarendon Bold, **Problem:** Negative/Positive

5

Typeface: Clarendon Bold, **Problem:** Negative/Positive

6

Typeface: Clarendon Bold, **Problem:** Negative/Positive

7

Typeface: Clarendon Bold, **Problem:** Negative/Positive

8

Typeface: Clarendon Bold, **Problem:** Negative/Positive

9

Typeface: Clarendon Bold, **Problem:** Negative/Positive

10

Typeface: Clarendon Bold, **Problem:** Negative/Positive

11

Typeface: Clarendon Bold, **Problem:** Negative/Positive

12

Typeface: Clarendon Bold, **Problem:** Negative/Positive

1

Typeface: Caslon Bold, **Problem:** Scale

2

Typeface: Ultra Bodoni, **Problem:** Playful

3

Typeface: Caslon Bold, **Problem:** Scale

4

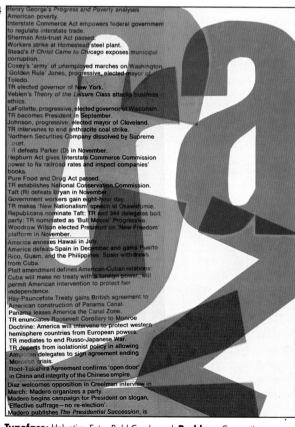

Typeface: Helvetica Extra Bold Condensed, **Problem:** Congestion

1. ROGER CAMP
2. LISA MAZUR
3. ALEKSANDR PUCHLIK
4. MIN-HUI CHANG
5. ROGER CAMP
6. COSTANZA PUGLISI
7. STEPHANIE ARCULLI
8. SHANA SOBEL
9. JEFF SCHULZ
10. LAUREN CAIATI
11. HANOCH PIVEN
12. KOBY CAULY
13. SHARON HAREL
14. DANIELA BARCELÓ
15. HANOCH PIVEN
16. KOBY CAULY

5

Typeface: Helvetica Extra Bold Condensed, **Problem:** Congestion

6

Typeface: Helvetica Extra Bold Condensed, **Problem:** Congestion

7

Typeface: Helvetica Extra Bold Condensed, **Problem:** Congestion

8

Typeface: Helvetica Extra Bold Condensed, **Problem:** Congestion

9

Typeface: Ultra Bodoni, **Problem:** Playful

10

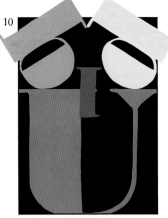

Typeface: Ultra Bodoni, **Problem:** Playful

11

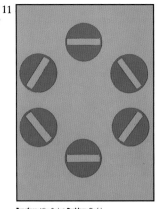

Typeface: Ultra Bodoni, **Problem:** Playful

12

Typeface: Ultra Bodoni, **Problem:** Playful

13

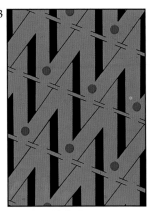

Typeface: Bodoni Bold, **Problem:** Pattern

14

Typeface: Bodoni Bold, **Problem:** Pattern

15

Typeface: Bodoni Bold, **Problem:** Pattern

16

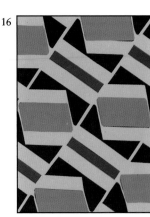

Typeface: Bodoni Bold, **Problem:** Pattern

DESIGNING WITH TYPE SOLUTIONS:

1

Typeface: Caslon Bold, **Problem:** Scale

2

Typeface: Ultra Bodoni, **Problem:** Playful

3
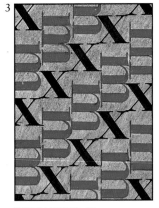
Typeface: Bodoni Bold, **Problem:** Pattern

4

Typeface: Clarendon Bold, **Problem:** Negative/Positive

5

Typeface: Bodoni Bold, **Problem:** Pattern

6
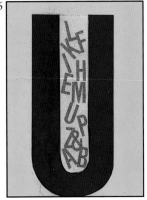
Typeface: Helvetica Extra Bold Condensed, **Problem:** Congestion

7

Typeface: Futura Black, **Problem:** Tension

8

Typeface: Bodoni Bold, **Problem:** Pattern

9
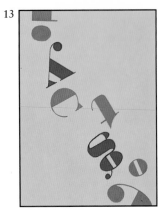
Typeface: Ultra Bodoni, **Problem:** Playful

10
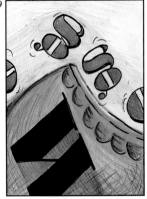
Typeface: Bodoni Bold, **Problem:** Pattern

11

Typeface: Futura Black, **Problem:** Tension

12

Typeface: Caslon Bold, **Problem:** Scale

13

Typeface: Ultra Bodoni, **Problem:** Playful

14

Typeface: Clarendon Bold, **Problem:** Negative/Positive

15

Typeface: Ultra Bodoni, **Problem:** Playful

16

Typeface: Ultra Bodoni, **Problem:** Playful

18

19

Typeface: Ultra Bodoni, **Problem:** Playful

Typeface: Futura Black, **Problem:** Tension

Typeface: Bodoni Bold, **Problem:** Pattern

21

Typeface: Clarendon Bold, **Problem:** Negative/Positive

22

Typeface: Caslon Bold, **Problem:** Scale

Typeface: Helvetica Extra Bold Condensed, **Problem:** Congestion

PROBLEM: TYPOGRAPHIC PORTRAITS

A specific personality is described in the twelve designated areas that appear on the assignment sheet. Visualize the character of the person described. Then, using your whole name, part of your name, or your nickname, choose an appropriate typeface for each individual personality and carfully render your name in the given area. Consider the style of the typeface, the weight of the typeface, the size of the typeface, the letterspacing, and the use of upper and lower case characters. Give special attention to the actual size and placement of your name in the given area.

SPECIFICATIONS

Size: As indicated on assignment sheet.
Color: Black and white. (Color should be considered only if it is integral to your concept.)
Medium: Pencil or ink.
Limitation: All solutions must be hand-lettered. Press type is unacceptable.
Suggestions: Study the typefaces found in type specimen books before making your selections. Use a luciograph to increase or decrease your type solutions to desired size.

My name is	My name is	My name is
and I'm a chameleon	and I'm an acrobat	and I'm an amphibian

My name is	My name is	My name is
and I'm a linebacker for the New York Giants	and I'm a taxi driver	and I'm a T.V. Evangelist

My name is	My name is	My name is
and I have an allergy	and I live in Chernobyl, Russia	and I have the hiccups

My name is	My name is	My name is
and I'm accident prone	and I'm a magician	

TYPOGRAPHIC PORTRAITS PROBLEM:

A specific personality aspect is described in each of the twelve rectangles
on the assignment sheet. First, choose
an appropriate typeface that best expresses the characteristics of each individual; then, carefully render your
whole name, part of your name, or your
nickname, considering the typeface
style, letterspacing, and use of upper-
and lowercase characters. Pay particular
attention to the actual size and placement of your name in the rectangle.

Analysis: Typography is the definitive
tool for the graphic designer—most
problems can be solved within the con-
fines of this expressive idiom. Learning
to work with type expessively is the
goal of this problem.

Initial problem-solving impulses are
usually oriented toward the literal, but
designers must go beyond this point and
take a more conceptual approach. For
instance, the use of one's own name to
express each solution represents a limited language for solving such complex
issues, yet the conditions of the problem
dictate the art of implying or inferring,
which becomes the vehicle for solving
each individual problem. These subtle
design decisions bring each solution
to life.

Note: The presentation of twelve different problems increases the chance for
successful solutions. Even just one success is no small feat, for it can open the
door for future successes.

TYPOGRAPHIC PORTRAITS SOLUTIONS:

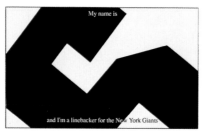

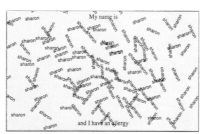

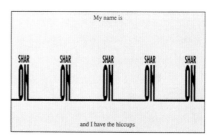

SHARON HAREL

YOUMI HEO

CARLOS BELTRÁN

CHIKA AZUMA

BETTE COWLES

TYPOGRAPHIC PORTRAITS SOLUTIONS:

1
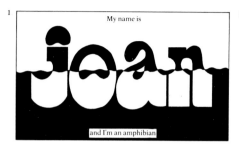
My name is
and I'm an amphibian

2

My name is
and I'm a magician

3
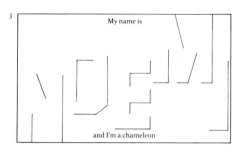
My name is
and I'm a chameleon

4
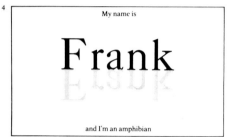
My name is
and I'm an amphibian

5

My name is
and I'm a magician

6

My name is
and I'm a chameleon

7
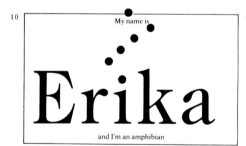
My name is
and I'm an amphibian

8

My name is
and I'm a magician

9
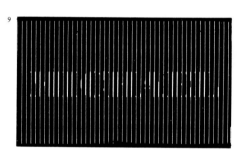

10
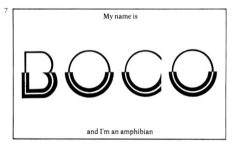
My name is
and I'm an amphibian

11
My name is

Instruction: Invisible ink. Iron, please.

and I'm a magician

12
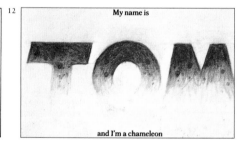
My name is
and I'm a chameleon

13

My name is
and I'm an amphibian

14

My name is
and I'm a magician

15

My name is
and I'm a chameleon

1. JOAN PALMER
2. IGNACIO RODRIGUEZ
3. NOEMI AYUSO
4. FRANK CASTALDI
5. JUDE DOMINIQUE

6. PERIEL TUNALIGIL
7. IP KWOK PO BOCO
8. TARA PATTERSON
9. MICHAEL RIVILIS
10. ERIKA BLEAKLEY

11. CLAUDIA GNADINGER
12. TOM GENERO
13. JUDE DOMINIQUE
14. JULIE WAGEMAN
15. EDWARD CHONG

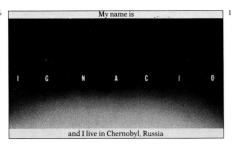

My name is

I G N A C I O

and I live in Chernobyl, Russia

17

My name is

and I have an allergy

18

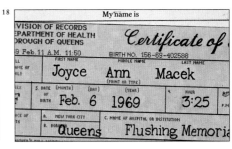

My name is

VISION OF RECORDS
EPARTMENT OF HEALTH
ROUGH OF QUEENS
9 Feb.11 A.M. 11:50   BIRTH NO. 156-69-402588
FIRST NAME   MIDDLE NAME   LAST NAME
Joyce   Ann   Macek
(PRINT OR TYPE)
5. DATE (MONTH) (DAY) (YEAR)   4. HOUR
Feb. 6   1969   3:25
A. NEW YORK CITY   C. NAME OF HOSPITAL OR INSTITUTION
B. BOROUGH
Queens   Flushing Memoria

Certificate of

My name is

CLAUDIA
GNAEDINGER

and I live in Chernobyl, Russia

20

My name is

HEIKE

and I have an allergy

21

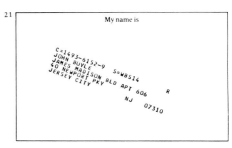

My name is

C=1493-6152-9   S=WB514
JOHN BOYLE
JAMES MADISON BLD APT 606
40 NEWPORT PKY   R
JERSEY CITY
NJ   07310

My name is

JOHN

and I live in Chernobyl, Russia

23

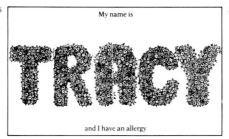

My name is

JOHN

and I have an allergy

24

My name is

雅 珊

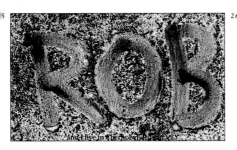

My name is

ROB

and I live in Chernobyl, Russia

26

My name is

TRACY

and I have an allergy

27

My name is

JON
DUEDE

My name is

NOEM

and I live in Chernobyl, Russia

29

My name is

and I have an allergy

30

HELLO
my name is

Demian Fore

and I don't like this assignment

16. IGNACIO RODRIGUEZ
17. TED DEUTERMANN
18. JOYCE MACEK
19. CLAUDIA GNADINGER
20. HEIKE UDES

21. JOHN BOYLE
22. CHRISTOPHER J. ROCCO
23. CHRISTOPHER J. ROCCO
24. MIRANDA MUSHFIQA NG
25. ROB CARDUCCI

26. TRACY WETSTEIN
27. JON DUEDE
28. NOEMI AYUSO
29. DONNA ELLIOTT
30. DEMIAN FORE

TYPOGRAPHIC PORTRAITS SOLUTIONS:

1
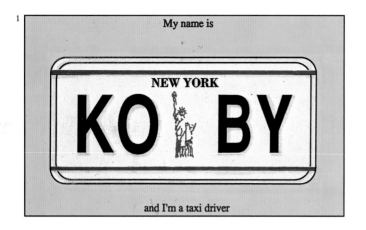
My name is
NEW YORK
KOBY
and I'm a taxi driver

2
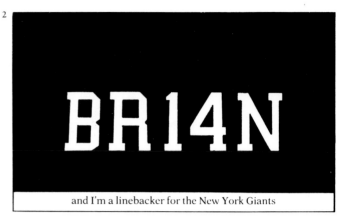
BR14N
and I'm a linebacker for the New York Giants

3

My name is
¡¡\S*!¡f—2;¡\S*
and I'm a taxi driver

4

My name is
and I'm a linebacker for the New York Giants

5

My name is
BOOL
and I'm a taxi driver

6
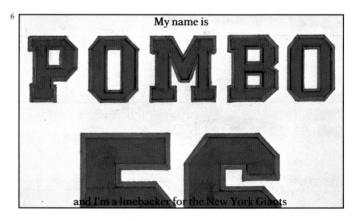
My name is
POMBO
56
and I'm a linebacker for the New York Giants

1. KOBY CAULY
2. BRIAN KELLY
3. TRACY WETSTEIN
4. TED DEUTERMANN
5. JULIE WAGEMAN
6. CARIN POMBO

7

My name is

Michelle and I'm a chameleon

8

My name is

and I'm an acrobat

9

My name is

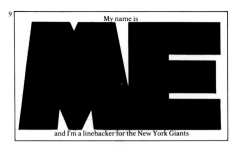

and I'm a linebacker for the New York Giants

10

My name is

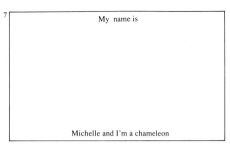

and I have an allergy

11

My name is

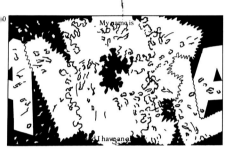

and I have an allergy

12

My name is

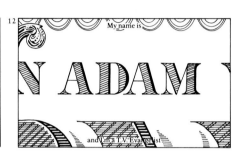

and I'm a T.V. Evangelist

13

My name is

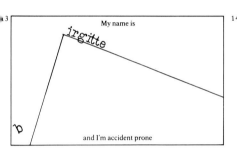

and I'm accident prone

14

15

My name is

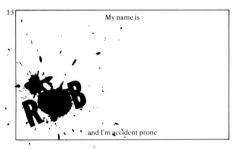

and I'm accident prone

16

and I have an allergy

17

My name is

and I'm a taxi driver

18

My name is

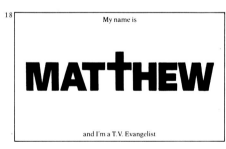

and I'm a T.V. Evangelist

ROAD SIGN

Immediacy in communication is the primary function of the road sign. In the (12) twelve yellow areas indicated below, graphically depict the intent of each road sign. Execute each solution in black as a finished piece. If the concept dictates, the use of color is permissible. On the reverse side create your own road sign.

PROBLEM

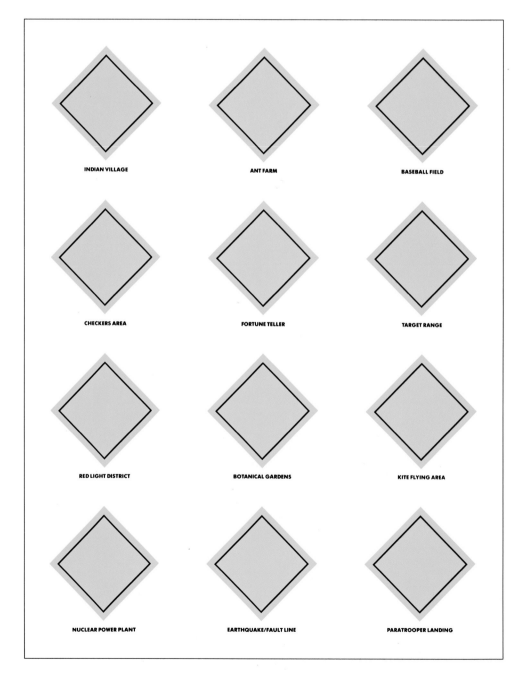

INDIAN VILLAGE

ANT FARM

BASEBALL FIELD

CHECKERS AREA

FORTUNE TELLER

TARGET RANGE

RED LIGHT DISTRICT

BOTANICAL GARDENS

KITE FLYING AREA

NUCLEAR POWER PLANT

EARTHQUAKE/FAULT LINE

PARATROOPER LANDING

ROAD SIGN PROBLEM:

Immediate, practical communication is the primary function of a road sign. With this in mind, graphically depict the subject indicated for each of the twelve road signs on the assignment sheet. Execute each solution as a finished piece in black; if the concept dictates, use of an additional color is permissible. On the back of the assignment sheet, create your own road sign depicting another subject and title it accordingly.

Analysis: This problem is a vehicle for simplicity and personalization. The intent is to inspire personal expression by giving each sign a unique life of its own. The familiar context suggests a traditional idiom, while the nonsensical topics allow for uninhibited design exploration and the opportunity to play; the parameters offer an opportunity to transcend the road sign's functional aspects through the creation of a personal statement in the name of design exploration.

ROAD SIGN SOLUTIONS:

1. PATRICK SUTHERLAND
2. THOMAS HARVEY
3. TARA PATTERSON
4. MIKKO MERONEN
5. ANDREW WALLACE
6. DALE SUTPHEN
7. JOSEPH FELIX
8. KLAUS GANER JOHANSEN
9. PETER DELORENZO
10. KOBY CAULY
11. STEVEN LAM
12. BETTE COWLES

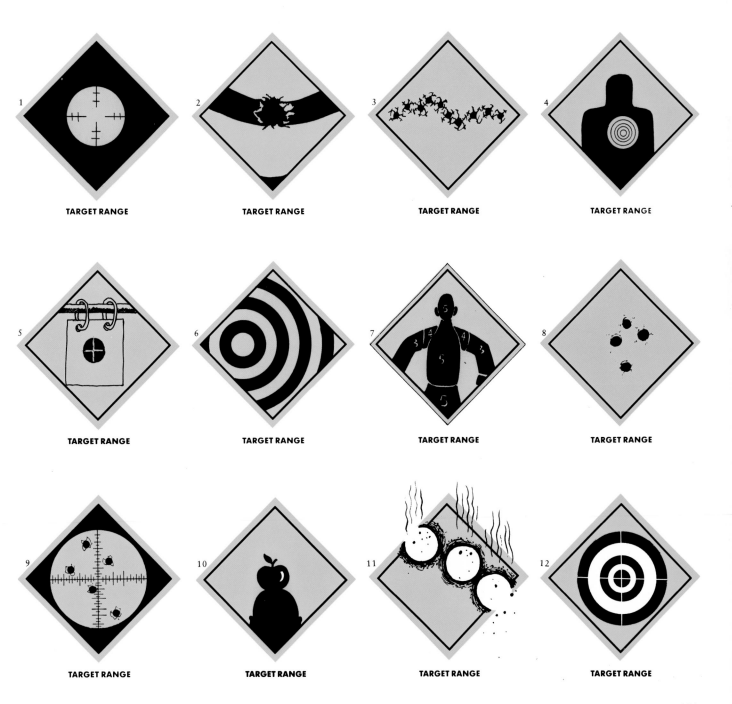

1   **TARGET RANGE**
2   **TARGET RANGE**
3   **TARGET RANGE**
4   **TARGET RANGE**

5   **TARGET RANGE**
6   **TARGET RANGE**
7   **TARGET RANGE**
8   **TARGET RANGE**

9   **TARGET RANGE**
10   **TARGET RANGE**
11   **TARGET RANGE**
12   **TARGET RANGE**

ROAD SIGN SOLUTIONS:

Solutions 13 through 16 are individual subjects created by students (the last condition of the assignment).

Solution 13 is a personal morse code message, which reads: "Happy Easter Richard, April 1990."

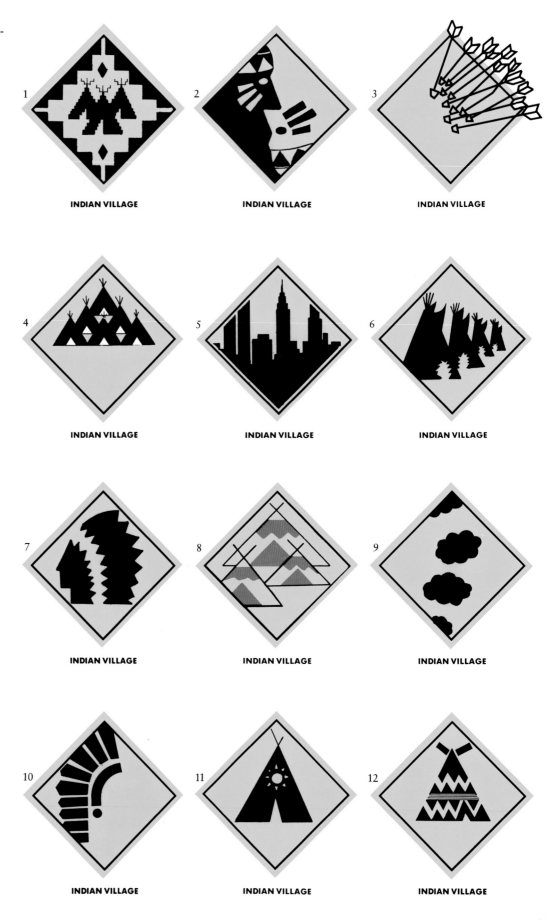

1 INDIAN VILLAGE

2 INDIAN VILLAGE

3 INDIAN VILLAGE

4 INDIAN VILLAGE

5 INDIAN VILLAGE

6 INDIAN VILLAGE

7 INDIAN VILLAGE

8 INDIAN VILLAGE

9 INDIAN VILLAGE

10 INDIAN VILLAGE

11 INDIAN VILLAGE

12 INDIAN VILLAGE

13. MORSE CODE MESSAGE
14. BIRD SANCTUARY
15. DANGEROUS INTERSECTION
16. PEDESTRIAN CROSSING

ROAD SIGN SOLUTIONS:

1

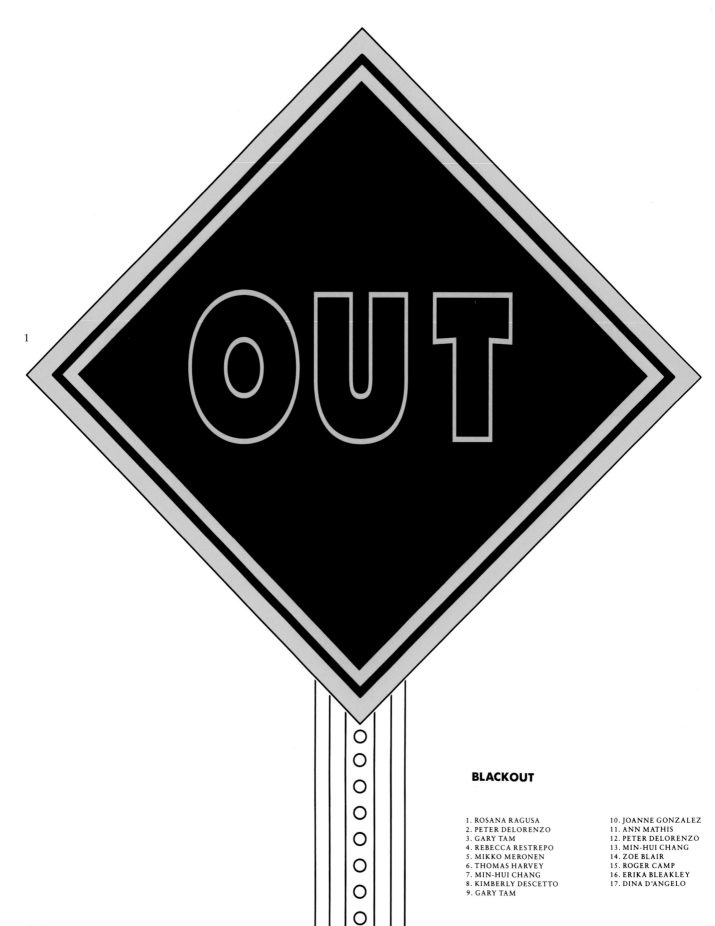

BLACKOUT

1. ROSANA RAGUSA
2. PETER DELORENZO
3. GARY TAM
4. REBECCA RESTREPO
5. MIKKO MERONEN
6. THOMAS HARVEY
7. MIN-HUI CHANG
8. KIMBERLY DESCETTO
9. GARY TAM

10. JOANNE GONZALEZ
11. ANN MATHIS
12. PETER DELORENZO
13. MIN-HUI CHANG
14. ZOE BLAIR
15. ROGER CAMP
16. ERIKA BLEAKLEY
17. DINA D'ANGELO

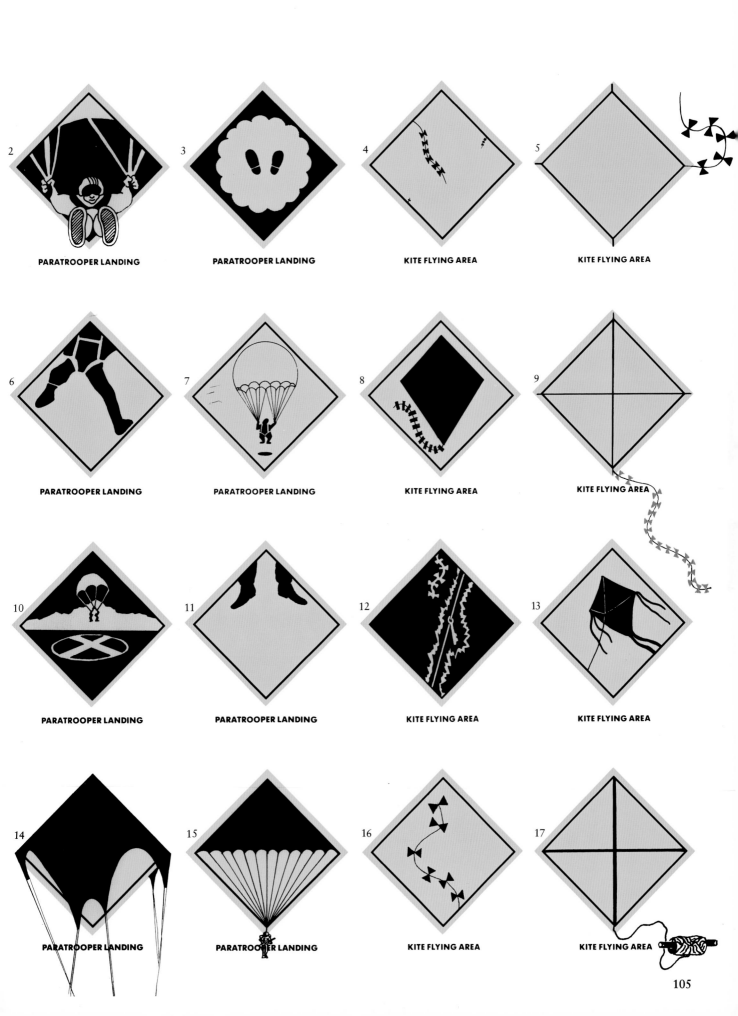

2 PARATROOPER LANDING

3 PARATROOPER LANDING

4 KITE FLYING AREA

5 KITE FLYING AREA

6 PARATROOPER LANDING

7 PARATROOPER LANDING

8 KITE FLYING AREA

9 KITE FLYING AREA

10 PARATROOPER LANDING

11 PARATROOPER LANDING

12 KITE FLYING AREA

13 KITE FLYING AREA

14 PARATROOPER LANDING

15 PARATROOPER LANDING

16 KITE FLYING AREA

17 KITE FLYING AREA

1 ○ FORTUNE TELLER

2 FORTUNE TELLER

3 RED LIGHT DISTRICT

4 RED LIGHT DISTRICT

5 FORTUNE TELLER

6 FORTUNE TELLER

7 RED LIGHT DISTRICT

8 RED LIGHT DISTRICT

9 FORTUNE TELLER

10 FORTUNE TELLER

11 RED LIGHT DISTRICT

12 RED LIGHT DISTRICT

13 FORTUNE TELLER

14 FORTUNE TELLER

15 RED LIGHT DISTRICT

16 RED LIGHT DISTRICT

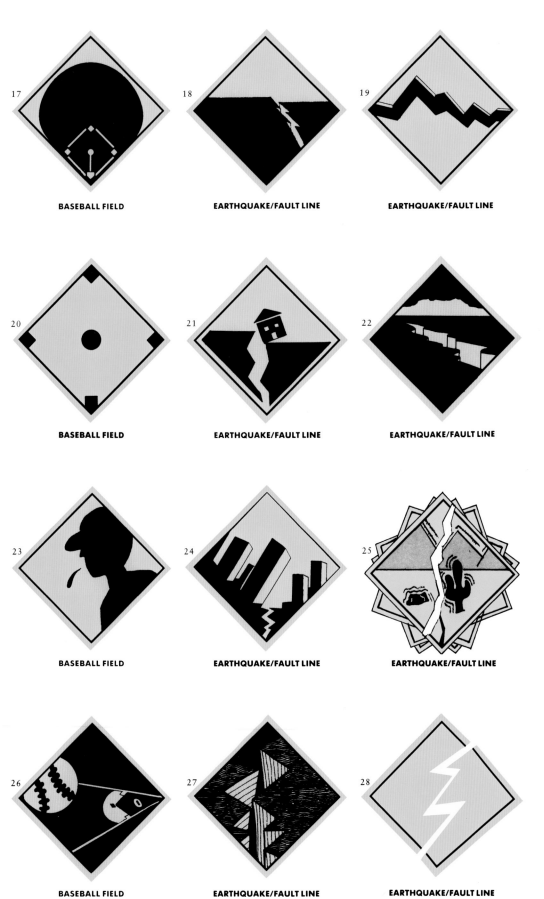

17

BASEBALL FIELD

18

EARTHQUAKE/FAULT LINE

19

EARTHQUAKE/FAULT LINE

20

BASEBALL FIELD

21

EARTHQUAKE/FAULT LINE

22

EARTHQUAKE/FAULT LINE

23

BASEBALL FIELD

24

EARTHQUAKE/FAULT LINE

25

EARTHQUAKE/FAULT LINE

26

BASEBALL FIELD

27

EARTHQUAKE/FAULT LINE

28

EARTHQUAKE/FAULT LINE

1. JONATHAN REED
2. LISA MAZUR
3. ROGER CAMP
4. DARYL CHEANG
5. DOUGLAS EISENGREIN
6. ANN MATHIS
7. DALE SUTPHEN
8. PETER DELORENZO
9. PATRICK RIVILIS
10. JOEL CLEMENT
11. KIMBERLY DESCETTO
12. MIN-HUI CHANG
13. PAMELA CANNON
14. ELIAS KOTSIAS
15. TOM GENERRO
16. SYLVIA FINZI
17. PATRICK RIVILIS
18. BETTE COWLES
19. MIKKO MERONEN
20. KIMBERLY SCHEREMETA
21. EDWARD CHIQUITUCTO
22. JOANNE GONZALEZ
23. PATRICK SUTHERLAND
24. PETER DELORENZO
25. ROGER CAMP
26. PETER DELORENZO
27. TONY MONTES
28. JONATHAN REED

ROAD SIGN SOLUTIONS:

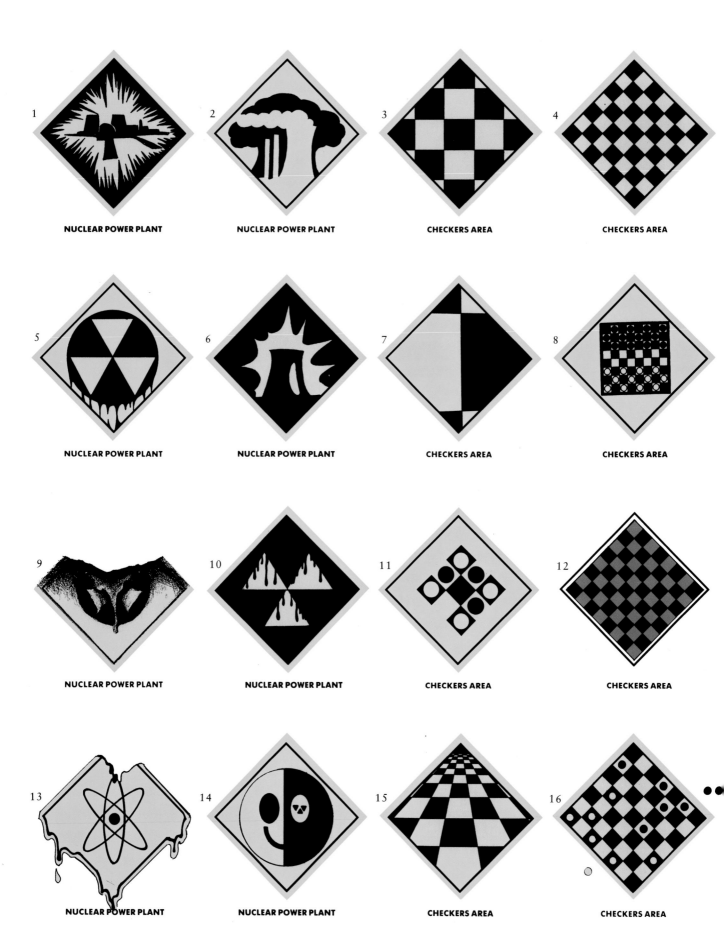

1 — NUCLEAR POWER PLANT

2 — NUCLEAR POWER PLANT

3 — CHECKERS AREA

4 — CHECKERS AREA

5 — NUCLEAR POWER PLANT

6 — NUCLEAR POWER PLANT

7 — CHECKERS AREA

8 — CHECKERS AREA

9 — NUCLEAR POWER PLANT

10 — NUCLEAR POWER PLANT

11 — CHECKERS AREA

12 — CHECKERS AREA

13 — NUCLEAR POWER PLANT

14 — NUCLEAR POWER PLANT

15 — CHECKERS AREA

16 — CHECKERS AREA

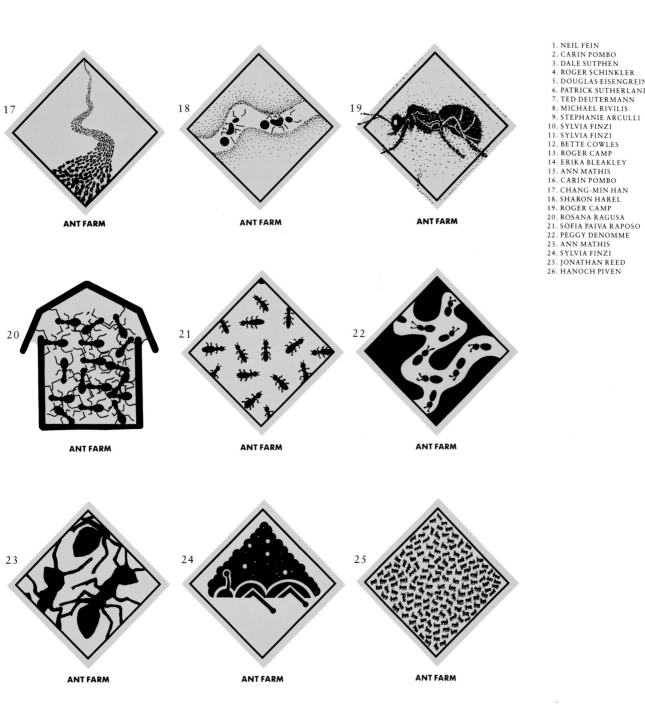

17
ANT FARM

18
ANT FARM

19
ANT FARM

1. NEIL FEIN
2. CARIN POMBO
3. DALE SUTPHEN
4. ROGER SCHINKLER
5. DOUGLAS EISENGREIN
6. PATRICK SUTHERLAND
7. TED DEUTERMANN
8. MICHAEL RIVILIS
9. STEPHANIE ARCULLI
10. SYLVIA FINZI
11. SYLVIA FINZI
12. BETTE COWLES
13. ROGER CAMP
14. ERIKA BLEAKLEY
15. ANN MATHIS
16. CARIN POMBO
17. CHANG-MIN HAN
18. SHARON HAREL
19. ROGER CAMP
20. ROSANA RAGUSA
21. SOFIA PAIVA RAPOSO
22. PEGGY DENOMME
23. ANN MATHIS
24. SYLVIA FINZI
25. JONATHAN REED
26. HANOCH PIVEN

20
ANT FARM

21
ANT FARM

22
ANT FARM

23
ANT FARM

24
ANT FARM

25
ANT FARM

26
ANT FARM

LIFE & DEATH

Passing a truck on the incorrect side could be the difference between life and death. Most trucks have "pass/do not pass" on the rear panels as a reminder to motorists. In an effort to make drivers more aware of this driving condition visualize a life/death situation to be executed on the rear panel of a truck. The theme of life/death encompasses a problem to be solved in two parts. Part one must accurately represent any subject, industrial object, animal, mineral, or vegetable. Part two must show its destruction. Part one must be completed on the left panel of the truck while part two must be completed on the right panel. Solutions may involve any subject matter as long as the two separate conditions of life and death are clear. Use the six smaller trucks for your preliminary sketches. Then select one and execute it on the larger truck to simulate a printed piece. There is no limitation on color or medium.

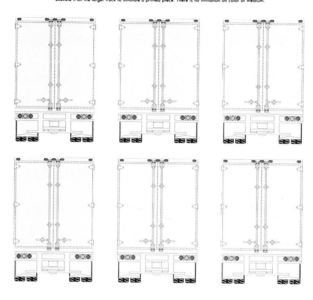

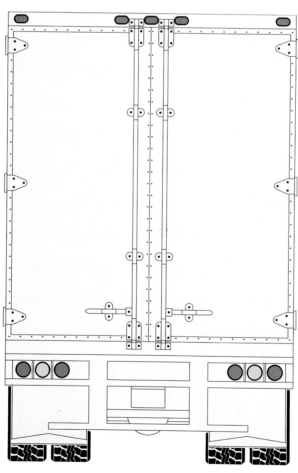

LIFE AND DEATH PROBLEM:

Choosing which side on which to pass a tractor-trailer on a busy highway could be the difference between life and death; most trucks have PASS/DO NOT PASS written on their lower rear panels as a reminder to motorists. With this in mind, visually interpret a life-and-death situation to be executed in two parts on the rear panels of the truck. Part one must accurately represent any industrial object, animal, mineral, or vegetable; part two must show its destruction or transformation. Part one must be completed on the left panel of the truck, and part two must be completed on the right panel. Solutions may involve any subject matter, as long as the two separate conditions of life and death are clear. Use the six smaller trucks on the assignment sheet for your preliminary sketches. Then select one and execute it on the larger truck to simulate a printed piece. There are no limitations on the use of color or media.

Analysis: The trucks are merely vehicles (no pun intended) for visually interpreting life-and-death situations. The idea is to make a personal statement, as opposed to a functional one, by extending a life–death concept into a meaningful graphic statement.

Note: To develop ideas for this problem, try writing a list. The written word often in turn suggests images, and the list can then be shortened to six preliminary topics. Eventually, designers may find they can apply this process to a broad range of problems and situations.

LIFE AND DEATH SOLUTIONS:

KELLY PORTERIEKO

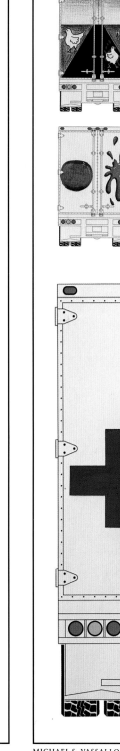

MICHAEL S. VASSALLO

112

1. KIMBERLY D. SCHEREMETA
2. KIMBERLY D. SCHEREMETA
3. CARIN POMBO

4. CHRISTOPHER ROCCO
5. SOFIA PAIVA RAPOSO
6. DARYL CHEANG

7. AEON STANFIELD
8. BRIAN GREENHALGH
9. PERIEL TUNALIGIL

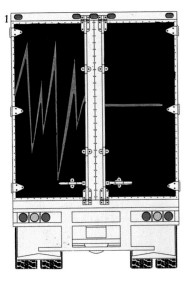

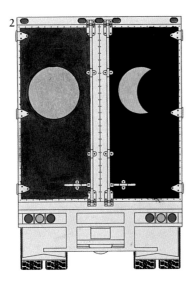

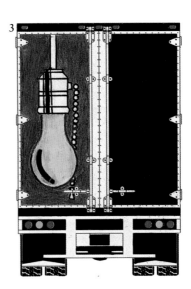

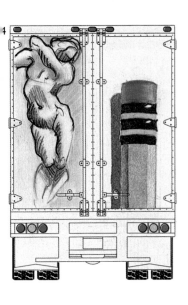

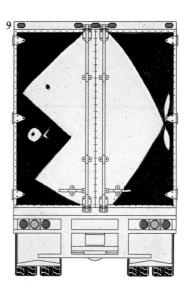

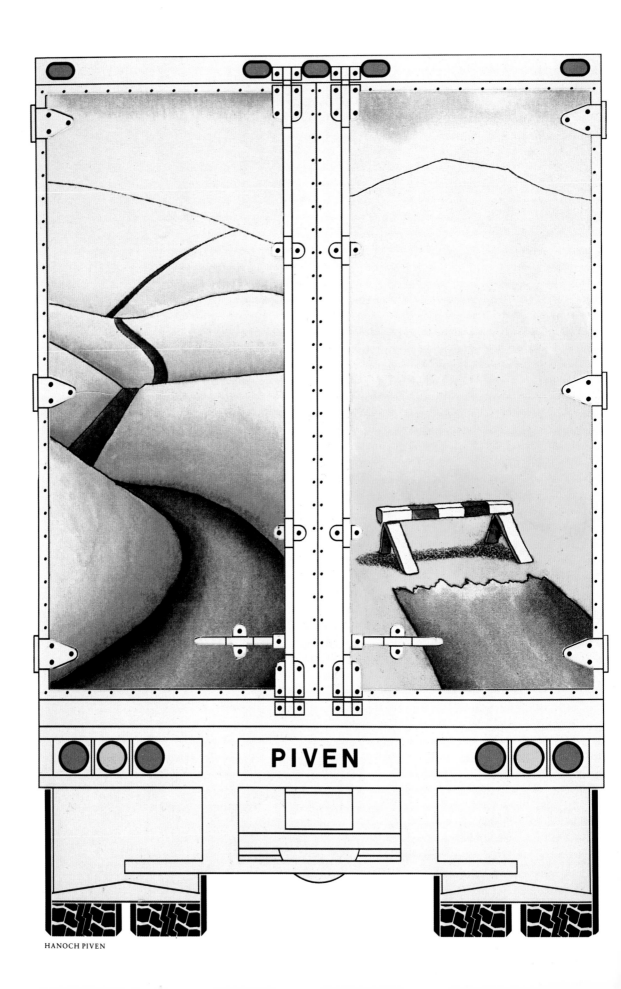

HANOCH PIVEN

1
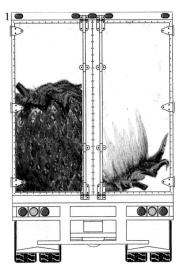

2
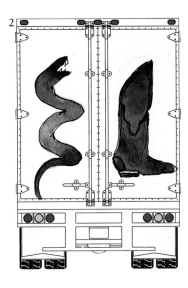

3

4
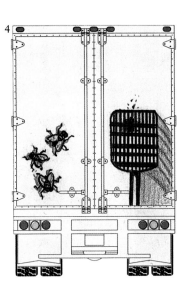

5
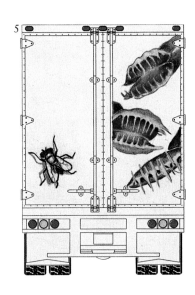

6

7
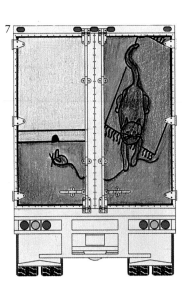

8
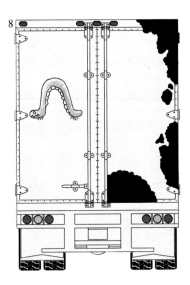

9
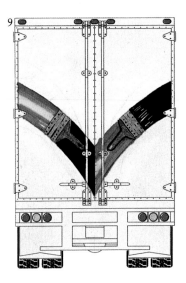

LIFE AND DEATH SOLUTIONS:

1–5. IP KWOK PO BOCO
6. GEORGALLIDES FRIXOS
7. KIMBERLY D. SCHEREMETA

8. ELIZABETH SLOANE
9. HANOCH PIVEN

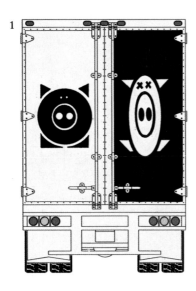

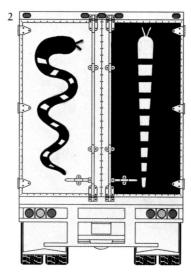

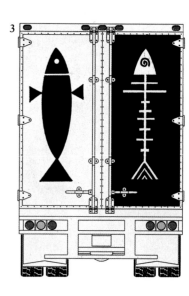

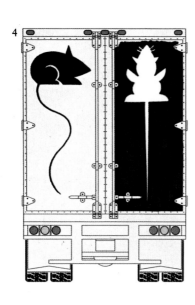

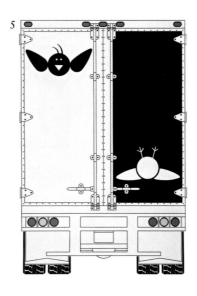

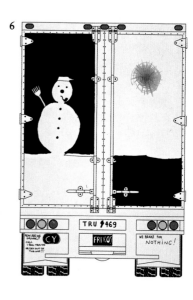

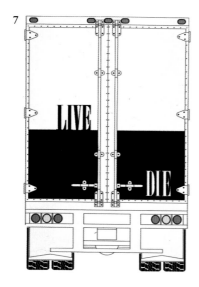

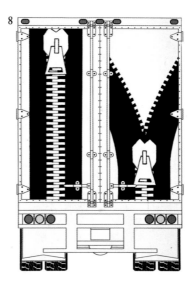

DOUGLAS DONELAN

CHIKA AZUMA

1–2. LYNETTE M. ZATOR
3. ALEXIS LOGOTHETIS
4. BRIAN GREENHALGH

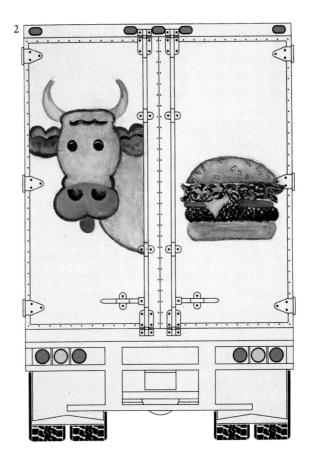

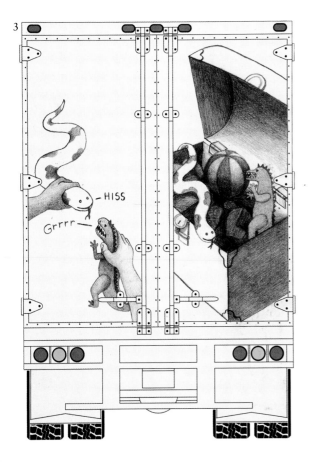

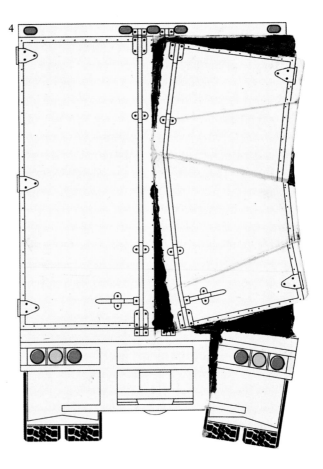

9025200637

The UPC mark is one of the most widely used symbols in the world, appearing on packaged goods, magazines, paperback books and other mass-produced products. Yet this image seen so frequently is often not seen at all. With this in mind, redesign the UPC symbol, making it visible by interpreting it as a personal, political, or social statement. The areas indicated below are to be used for preliminary drawings. When all eight sketches are completed, choose one and execute it as accurately as possible in the larger area. There are no limitations on medium or color.

UPC PROBLEM:

The Universal Product Code, or UPC, is one of the most widely used marks in the world, appearing on packaged foods, magazines, books, records, and other mass-produced products. Indeed, the UPC mark has become a symbol of consumerism throughout the world. But because this image is seen so frequently, it is almost always taken for granted and consequently not really seen at all—it has become part of the invisible fabric of our daily lives. With this in mind, redesign the UPC mark, making it visible once again by interpreting it as a personal, political, or social statement. The eight small areas indicated on the assignment sheet are to be used for preliminary drawings. When all the sketches are completed, choose one and execute it as accurately as possible in the larger area. There are no limitations on the use of color or media.

Analysis: The ubiquitous UPC mark serves as a point of departure for a design activity that calls for experimentation with this familiar image. As with the Road Sign Problem, the inherent familiarity of the subject gives a certain tangibility to the problem, but the success of the solution ultimately lies in the articulation of its graphic execution and formalistic concerns.

Notes: This problem affords a light, playful problem-solving approach, which prompts satirical, comical, and witty solutions for a designer's graphic vocabulary.

An innate aspect of the UPC Problem is that a double entendre comes into play, allowing the mark to maintain its identity while adopting new meanings. Again, this broadens a designer's skills and encourages simultaneous analyses in multiple contexts.

ULRIK HOLM MICHELSON

JACOB JOHNSSON

JOHN LUTTROPP

ANNETTE OVLISEN

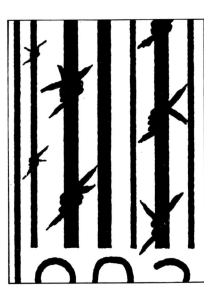

CLANDIA GNADINGER

JEANNETTE THORUP LARSEN

GLENN LEDOUX

MIKKEL HARTRIG ANDERSON

JOHN LUTTROPP

UPC SOLUTIONS:

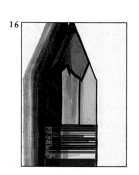

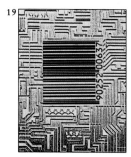

BRET HAINES

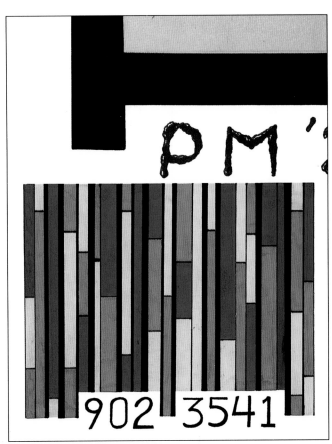

JONATHAN D. REED

NEIL RINDER

ALEXIS LOGOTHETIS

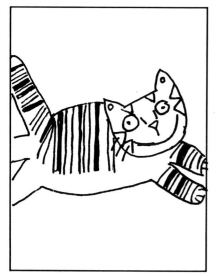

GRACE MARIE SCAGLIONE

ROSANA RAGUSA

JOHN LUTTROPP

90252 00637

MARTIN SCHELLER

STEIN-ARNE HOVE

MIKKEL HARTRIG ANDERSON

90252 00637

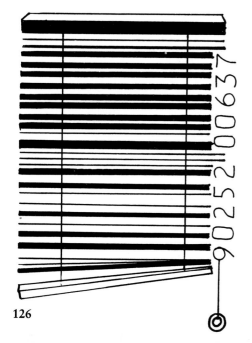

VIBEKE BENGSTON
Left: JEANNETTE THORUP LARSEN

MARIA RAMBO

 1

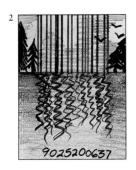 2

 3

 4

 5

 6

 7

 8

 9

 10

 11

 12

 13

 14

 15

 16

 17

 18

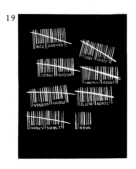 19

 20

SOUND PROBLEM: In the spaces provided below, graphically represent the sounds of the topics indicated. In each of the nine problems, carefully consider the character of the sound, its tempo, volume, duration, context, and color. Also consider working abstractly or typographically. In the untitled space in the lower right hand corner, choose your own subject and visualize its sound. Title it on the reverse side of the assignment sheet.

CAR CRASH

CLOCK

TYPEWRITER

CONVERSATION BETWEEN OVERBEARING
FATHER AND SHY DAUGHTER

CONVERSATION BETWEEN A TUBA AND
A FLUTE

CONVERSATION BETWEEN USA AND USSR

BUMBLEBEES MAKING LOVE

JAZZ BAND JAMMING PIANO, BASS FIDDLE,
DRUMS, GUITAR AND TRUMPET

SOUND PROBLEM I:

In the spaces provided, graphically represent the sounds indicated below each space on the assignment sheet. In each case, carefully consider the character of the sound in terms of its tempo, volume, duration, context, and "color." Consider working abstractly, metaphorically, or typographically. For the space in the lower right corner, choose your own subject and graphically visualize its sound. Title it on the reverse side of the assignment sheet. There are no limitations on the use of color or media.

Analysis: Although literal problem solving has its place in design, a graphic vocabulary must be expanded beyond this simple narrative voice. The intent of the Sound Problem is to spur a designer past the initial predictable response of literalism, to investigate other avenues of problem solving and more sophisticated approaches. An extensive graphic design vocabulary is better equipped to solve complex problems using metaphor, symbolism, abstraction, or typography; the conditions of this problem encourages a designer in this direction.

Note: Each solution has the support of a copy line, which gives the viewer a reference point for understanding the nine individual segments of the assignment. The relationship between copy and image becomes an integral part of each solution as the two elements play off one another to capture the viewer's attention. Any necessary information not supplied by the copy or graphics is contributed by the viewer comprehending the piece. Encouraging this relationship between viewer and communication piece is a primary objective of the Sound Problem.

SOUND PROBLEM: In the spaces provided below, graphically represent the sounds of the topics indicated. In each of the (9) nine problems, carefully consider the character of the sound, its tempo, volume, duration, context and color. Also consider working abstractly or typographically. In the untitled space in the lower right hand corner, choose your own subject and visualize its sound. Title it on the reverse side of the assignment sheet.

CAR CRASH

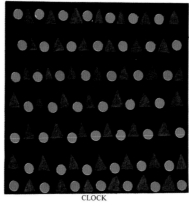

CLOCK

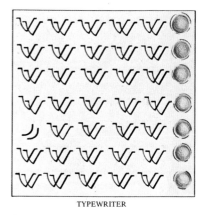

TYPEWRITER

CONVERSATION BETWEEN OVERBEARING
FATHER AND SHY DAUGHTER

CONVERSATION BETWEEN A TUBA AND
A FLUTE

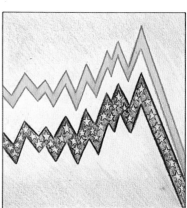

CONVERSATION BETWEEN USA AND USSR

BUMBLEBEES MAKING LOVE

JAZZ BAND JAMMING PIANO, BASS FIDDLE,
DRUMS, GUITAR AND TRUMPET

PROBLEMS : SOLUTIONS SERIES

JEAN CRONIN

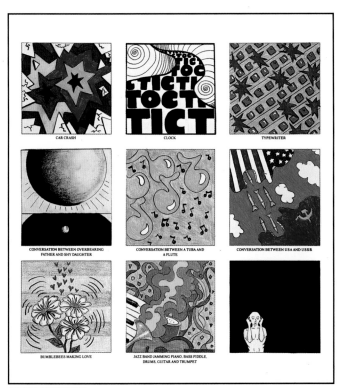

KELLY PORTERIEKO

MELISSA S. SISON

MATTHEW PAUL MAUS

ERIC C. KING

SOUND SOLUTIONS:

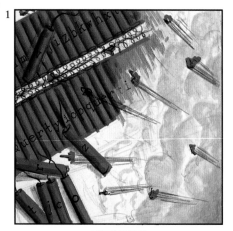

1

TYPEWRITER

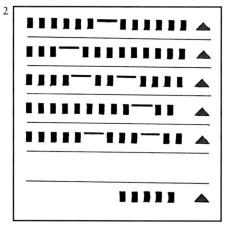

2

TYPEWRITER

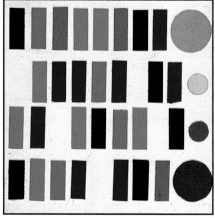

3

TYPEWRITER

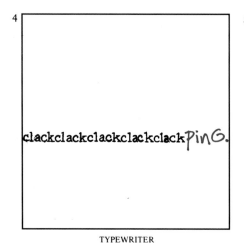

4

clackclackclackclackclack piNG.

TYPEWRITER

5

TYPEWRITER

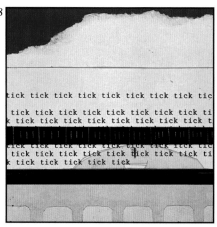

6

The quick brown fox jumped over the lazy dog.
The quick brown fox jumped over the lazy dog.
The quick brown fox jumped over the lazy dog.
The quick brown fox jumped over the lazy dog.

TYPEWRITER

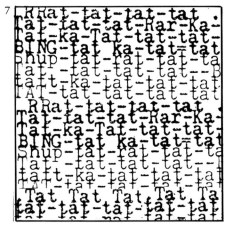

7

TYPEWRITER

8

TYPEWRITER

9

TYPEWRITER

TYPEWRITER

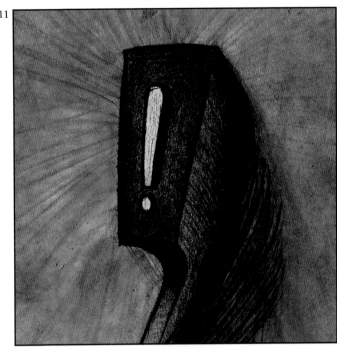

TYPEWRITER

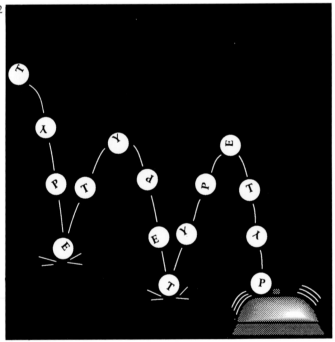

TYPEWRITER

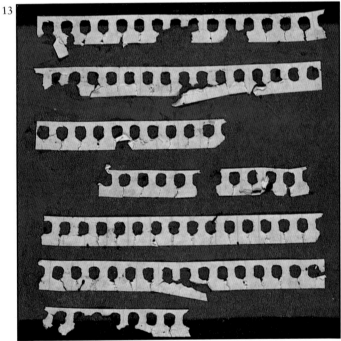

TYPEWRITER

133

SOUND SOLUTIONS:

1. CAR CRASH

2. CAR CRASH

3. CAR CRASH

4. CAR CRASH

5. CAR CRASH

6. CAR CRASH

7. CAR CRASH

8. CAR CRASH

9. CAR CRASH

1. MARC MASCIOVECCHIO
2. LISA MAZUR
3. MARTIN MOSER
4. CLAUDIA GNADINGER
5. EVA DEAK
6. CHENG-YI HSIAO

134

10 HARP

11 CONVERSATION AT AN ITALIAN FAMILY DINNER

12 MISTAKE

13 RECORD BEING SCRATCHED

14 DEATH

15 RUNNING WATER

16 AN EMPTY STOMACH

17 SOUND OF SPRING

18 CAT CAUGHT IN A BEAR TRAP

SOUND SOLUTIONS:

CONVERSATION BETWEEN OVERBEARING
FATHER AND SHY DAUGHTER

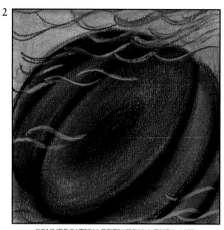

CONVERSATION BETWEEN A TUBA AND
A FLUTE

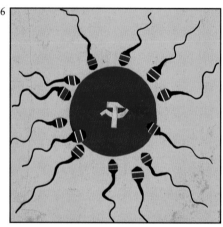

CONVERSATION BETWEEN USA AND USSR

CONVERSATION BETWEEN OVERBEARING
FATHER AND SHY DAUGHTER

CONVERSATION BETWEEN A TUBA AND
A FLUTE

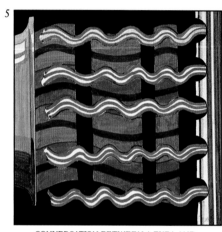

CONVERSATION BETWEEN USA AND USSR

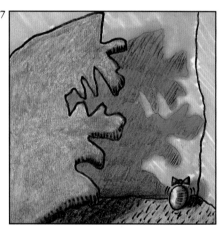

CONVERSATION BETWEEN OVERBEARING
FATHER AND SHY DAUGHTER

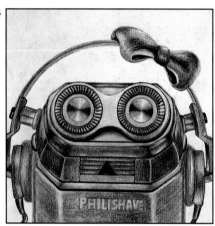

CONVERSATION BETWEEN A TUBA AND
A FLUTE

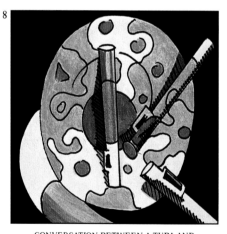

CONVERSATION BETWEEN USA AND USSR

CONVERSATION BETWEEN USA AND USSR

CONVERSATION BETWEEN USA AND USSR

CONVERSATION BETWEEN USA AND USSR

CONVERSATION BETWEEN USA AND USSR

1. DAVID BERLIN
2. PEGGY DENOMME
3. RONALD CIANFAGLIONE
4. CHENG-YI HSIAO
5. GEORGE MARISCAL
6. HANOCH PIVEN
7. STEVE PARISO
8. STEVE PARISO
9. SUSAN GENDLER
10. CHANG-MIN HAN
11. JOE ALLEGRETTI
12. BETTE COWLES
13. JOYCE MACEK

SOUND SOLUTIONS:

BUMBLEBEES MAKING LOVE

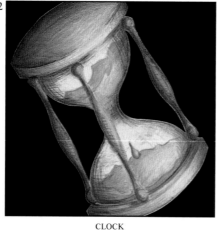

CLOCK

JAZZ BAND JAMMING: PIANO, BASS FIDDLE, DRUMS, GUITAR AND TRUMPET

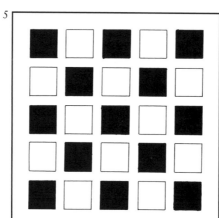

BUMBLEBEES MAKING LOVE

CLOCK

JAZZ BAND JAMMING: PIANO, BASS FIDDLE, DRUMS, GUITAR AND TRUMPET

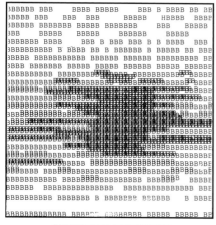

BUMBLEBEES MAKING LOVE

CLOCK

JAZZ BAND JAMMING: PIANO, BASS FIDDLE, DRUMS, GUITAR AND TRUMPET

1. MARIA RAMBO
2. STEPHANIE ARCULLI
3. PATRICK D'ANGELO
4. LYNETTE MARIE ZATOR
5. MARTIN MOSER
6. JENNIFER JULIANO
7. STEPHANIE LOWRY
8. CHENG-YI HSIAO
9. MERCEDES CURUTCHET
10. CHRISTOPHER R. JENNINGS

138

JAZZ BAND JAMMING: PIANO, BASS FIDDLE,
DRUMS, GUITAR AND TRUMPET

Even more so than the other problems in this section of the book, the Sound Problem opens up the question, *What is graphic design?* This problem is so limitless, with so many possible approaches and so few parameters, that some may question whether it truly falls within the context of graphic design. But such a doubt implies that graphic design has a firm definition, an agreed-upon set of boundaries, when in fact this is not the case. To attempt to define graphic design in this way is to limit it, reduce it, minimize it. The Sound Problem attempts to do just the opposite.

Choose one of the following subjects and visually interpret it one hundred ways: paper bag, frog, gumball machine, ant, dandelion, manhole cover, sun, sneaker, or apple. Carefully consider the various graphic design principles—including cropping, touching, overlapping, and intersecting of forms, negative and positive relationships, composition, texture, scale, framal reference, illusory space, and color—to discover the language of graphic design. In the larger rectangle indicated on the assignment sheet, select what you consider your best solution and execute it in that area. Consider all techniques and approaches in solving this problem. There are no limitations on color or medium.

GRAPHIC DESIGN 101 PROBLEM:

Choose one of the following subjects and visually interpret it one hundred different ways: paper bag, frog, gumball machine, sneaker, manhole cover, sun, ant, dandelion, or apple. As you work, carefully consider the language of graphic design and the various graphic design principles, including cropping, touching, overlapping, and intersecting of forms, negative and positive relationships, composition, texture, scale, framal reference, illusory space, and color.

Select what you consider your best solution and execute it in the larger rectangle on the assignment sheet. Consider all techniques and approaches in solving this problem. There are no limitations on the use of color or media.

Analysis: In the professional world of graphic design, challenging problems often call for unique imagery. The problem of Graphic Design 101 encourages playing, risk taking, and experimentation. At the same time, the problem teaches endurance and resourcefulness—the requirement of trying to find so many preliminary ideas can be exhausting. This is the critical point in the assignment, when attention tends to wander and impatience begins to set in. By simply completing this demanding assignment, the designer begins to believe in his or her own possibilities.

Note: Selecting a successful solution from a large number of choices is in itself a very important aspect of the design process, and consequently appears in many of the assignments throughout this book. Editing—especially *self-editing*—is a critical skill that requires an inner sense or understanding of what attracts one's own attention (the most obvious barometer for assessing impacts on viewers' attentions) while keeping in mind the precise intent of the problem. Good editing skills reinforce good problem-solving skills, and vice versa.

Choose one of the following subjects and visually interpret it one hundred ways: paper bag, frog, gumball machine, ant, dandelion, manhole cover, sun, sneaker, or apple. Carefully consider the various graphic design principles—including cropping, touching, overlapping, and intersecting of forms, negative and positive relationships, composition, texture, scale, framal reference, illusory space, and color—to discover the language of graphic design. In the larger rectangle indicated on the assignment sheet, select what you consider your best solution and execute it in that area. Consider all techniques and approaches in solving this problem. There are no limitations on color or medium.

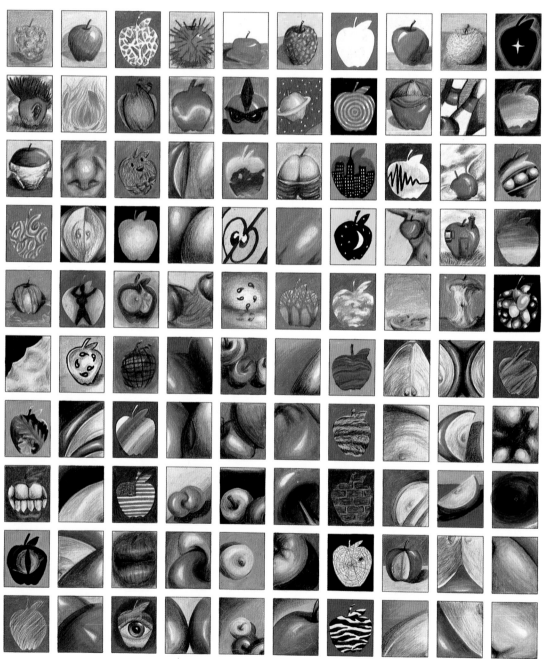

PROBLEMS : SOLUTIONS SERIES

LARESSA LUZNIAK

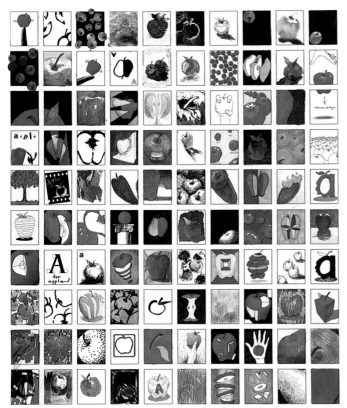

CALVIN CHU

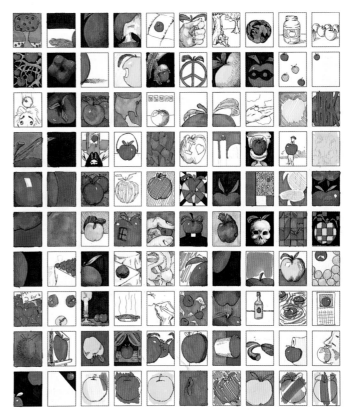

JOSEPH TIERNEY

BECKY NOCELLA

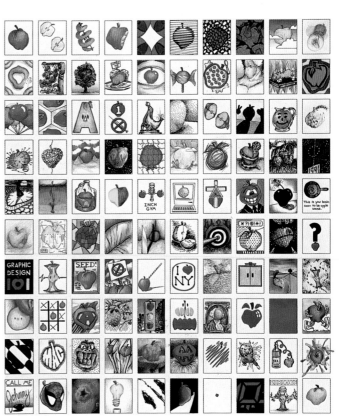

TODD MABREY

143

GRAPHIC DESIGN 101 SOLUTIONS:

PATRICK W. AQUINTEY

GENE DE CICCO

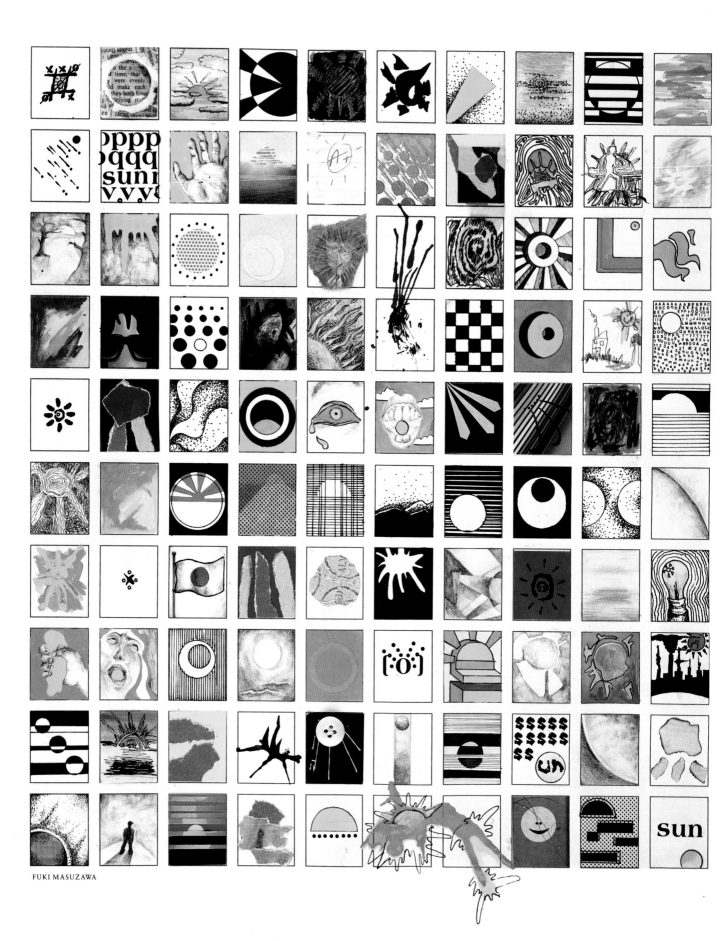

FUKI MASUZAWA

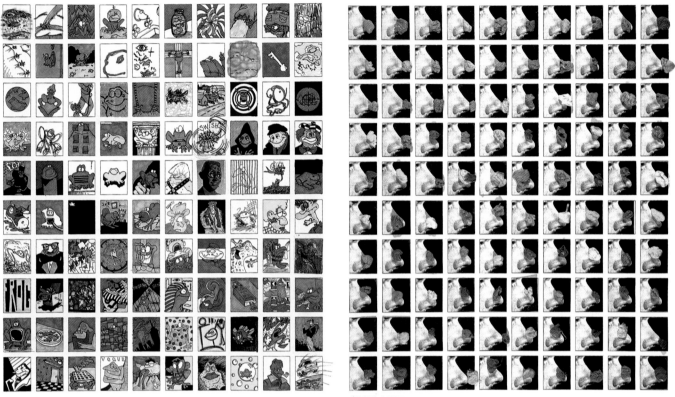

T.J. MILLER

SHANA SOBEL

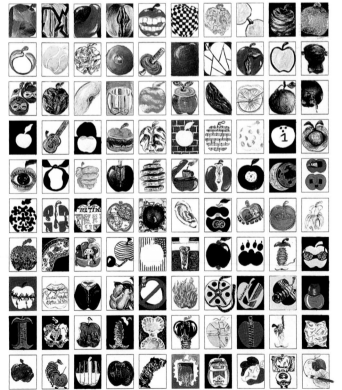

PEGGY FERRAND

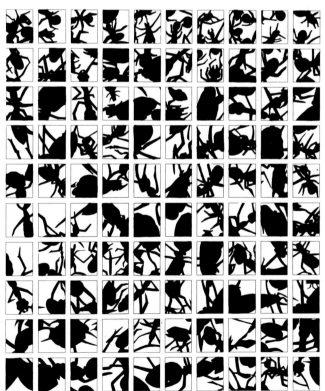

FRANK GALLO

147

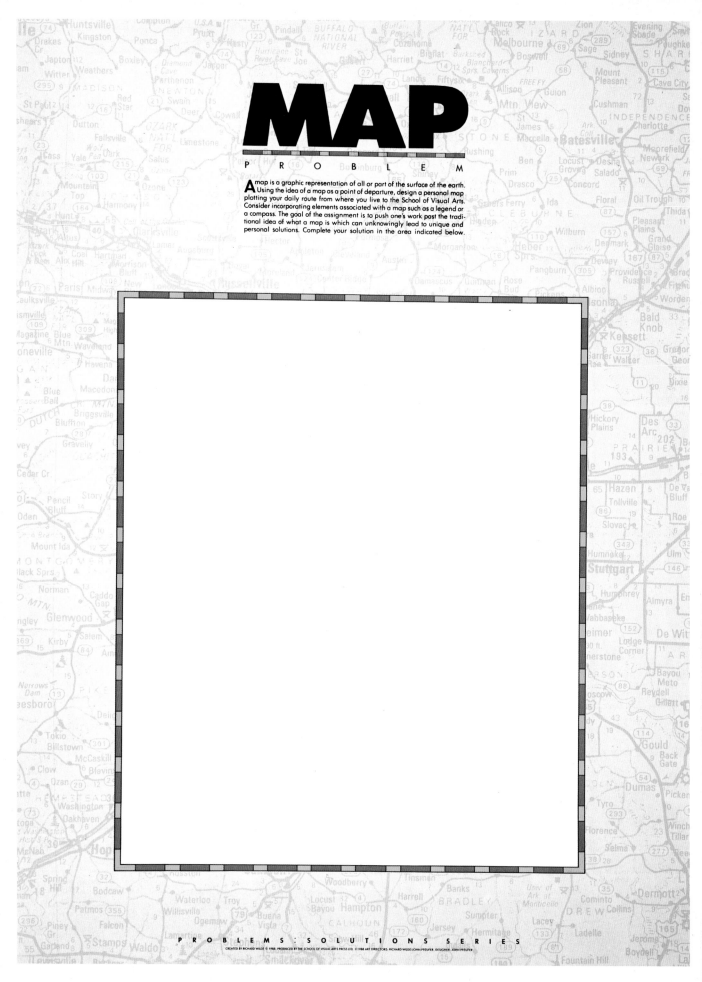

MAP

A map is a graphic representation of all or part of the surface of the earth. Using the idea of a map as a point of departure, design a personal map plotting your daily route from where you live to the School of Visual Arts. Consider incorporating elements associated with a map such as a legend or a compass. The goal of the assignment is to push one's work past the traditional idea of what a map is which can unknowingly lead to unique and personal solutions. Complete your solution in the area indicated below.

CREATED BY RICHARD WILDE © 1988. PRODUCED BY THE SCHOOL OF VISUAL ARTS PRESS LTD. ©1988 ART DIRECTORS: RICHARD WILDE/JOHN PFEUFER. DESIGNER: JOHN PFEUFER.

MAP PROBLEM:

By definition, a map is a flat-surfaced pictorial representation of the earth or the heavens. Using the idea of a map as a point of departure, chart your daily route from where you live to your school or job. Consider incorporating elements associated with maps, such as a legend, a compass, or visual topography. Execute your solution in the area indicated on the assignment sheet. There are no limitations on the use of color or media.

Analysis: The medium of a map, which can be understood as a graphic guide, is fertile ground for discovering and developing personal problem-solving strategies. By focusing on the charting and plotting of comings and goings and exploring all aspects of what a map can represent, personal travel experience can produce innovative design solutions that extend well beyond the traditional map concept.

Note: This problem's uniqueness lies in the connection between the two given points of a journey and the time-sequenced visual documentation that follows. The idea of what is actually being communicated (going from one place to another) is of secondary importance here—the critical aspect is not *what*, but *how*.

MAP SOLUTIONS:

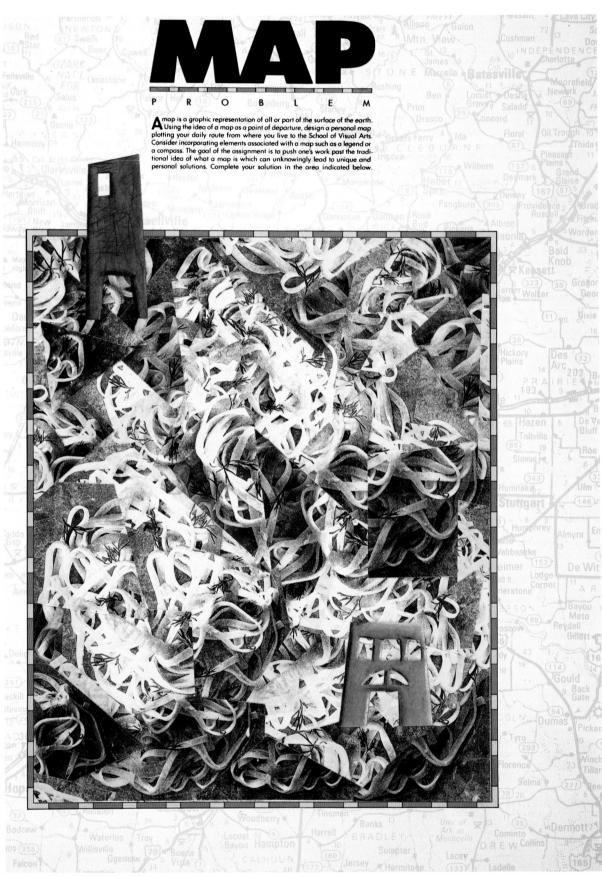

MAP
P R O B L E M

A map is a graphic representation of all or part of the surface of the earth. Using the idea of a map as a point of departure, design a personal map plotting your daily route from where you live to the School of Visual Arts. Consider incorporating elements associated with a map such as a legend or a compass. The goal of the assignment is to push one's work past the traditional idea of what a map is which can unknowingly lead to unique and personal solutions. Complete your solution in the area indicated below.

ROB CARDUCCI

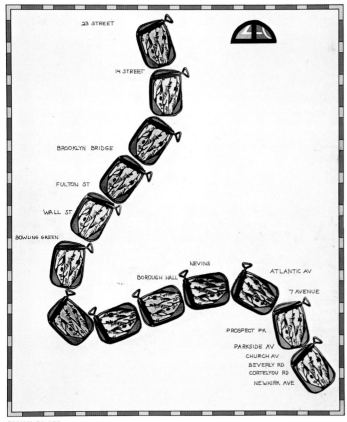

EMILY GRAFF

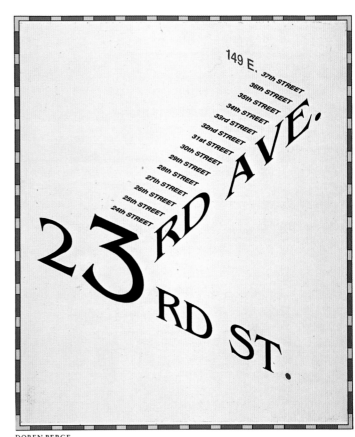

DOREN BERGE

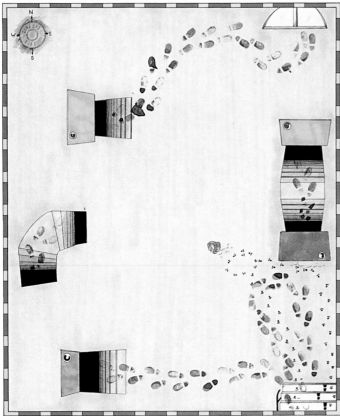

MIKKO MERONEN

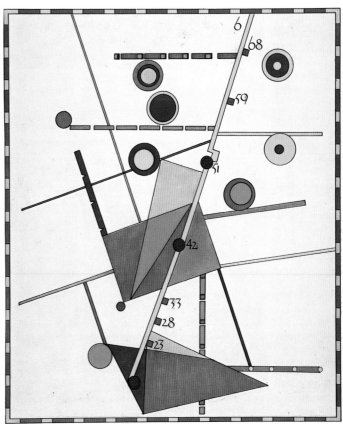

SYLVIA FINZI

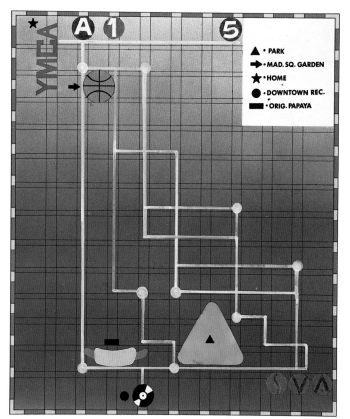

DOUG EISENGREIN

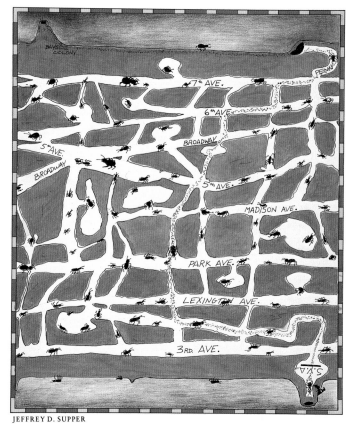

JEFFREY D. SUPPER

BRIAN GROSS

DAVID QUASHA

JEFF SCHULZ

153

Every day, either consciously or unconsciously, I sing songs to myself in my head as I ride the subway to school. On February 28, 1990 I made a note of what song was in my head when I reached each subway stop. This is the map of the day's ride:

86th. Street - " Praise God I'm Satisfied" - Blind Willie Johnson.

77th. Street - " Walking The Dog" - Rufus Thomas.

68th. Street - " Shake " - Otis Redding.

59th. Street - " Land Of 1,000 Dances " - Wilson Picket.

51st. Street - " I Thank You " - Sam & Dave.

42nd. Street - " This Is A Man's, Man's, Man's world " - The Residents.

34th. Street - " Its A Beautiful World " - Devo.

28th. Street - " Kawdy Korn " - Captain Beefheart.

23rd. Street - " Free Your Mind And Your Ass Will Follow " - Funkadelic.

ANTHONY MONTES

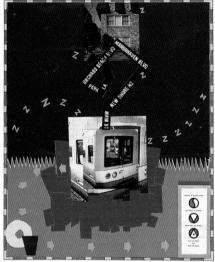

BETTE COWLES

AEON STANFIELD

PATRICK FRIGIOLA

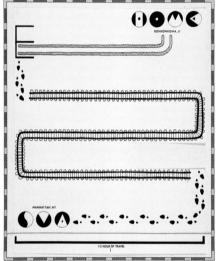

ANN MATHIS

TED DEUTERMANN

LISA MAZUR

ANGELA ESPOSITO

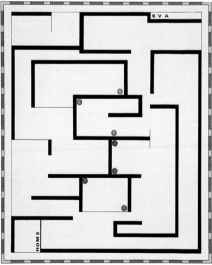

MIRANDA NG

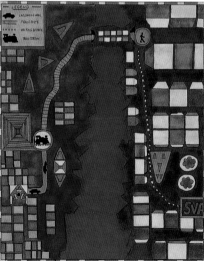

CHRISTOPHER CARROLL

155

Homage to André Breton

André Breton was a surrealist writer who made a study of the unconscious by experimenting with the phenomena of automatic writing.

In an attempt to expand your perception of the creative process and discover unconscious forms and images that have been buried beneath conventional appearances and habits, use the three small grid-like areas on the assignment sheet to create an image in the spirit of André Breton.

Begin by trying not to think about what you are doing. Just let your automatic functions take over, by letting them proceed as they wish. In a way, your final solution is not up to your normal way of solving problems, but from a deeper, more intuitive impulse. Let whatever happens, happen.

Use the larger area, at the bottom of the assignment sheet, to create your own personal solution by reverting to your usual way of working. Here you may impose your will to create whatever imagery, abstract or literal, you wish to explore.

There are no limitations on color or medium.

HOMAGE TO ANDRÉ BRETON
PROBLEM:

André Breton was a French surrealist poet who studied the unconscious by experimenting with the phenomenon of *automatic writing*. This assignment reflects and draws upon his methods.

In an attempt to expand your perception of the creative process and discover subconscious forms and images buried beneath conventional appearances and habits, use the three small, gridlike areas on the assignment sheet to create an image in the spirit of André Breton.

Try not to think about what you are doing—just let your automatic functions take over, letting them proceed as they wish. Your final solution will not come from your normal way of solving problems, but from a deeper, more intuitive impulse. So whatever happens, let it happen.

Use the larger area at the bottom of the assignment sheet to create your own personal solution by reverting to your usual way of working. Here you may impose your will to create whatever imagery, abstract or literal, you wish to explore.

There are no limitations on the use of color or media.

Analysis: This problem is given in the spirit of pure experimentation with the hope of catching a glimpse of other consciousness levels that are always present within us but rarely perceived. Touching the unknown is the beginning of the realization that there is much more to learn about one's own nature. This in itself is a most valuable lesson, and it can be summarized as follows: The more you know, the more you realize that you don't know much at all.

IP KWOK PO BOCO

HELEN ORTIZ

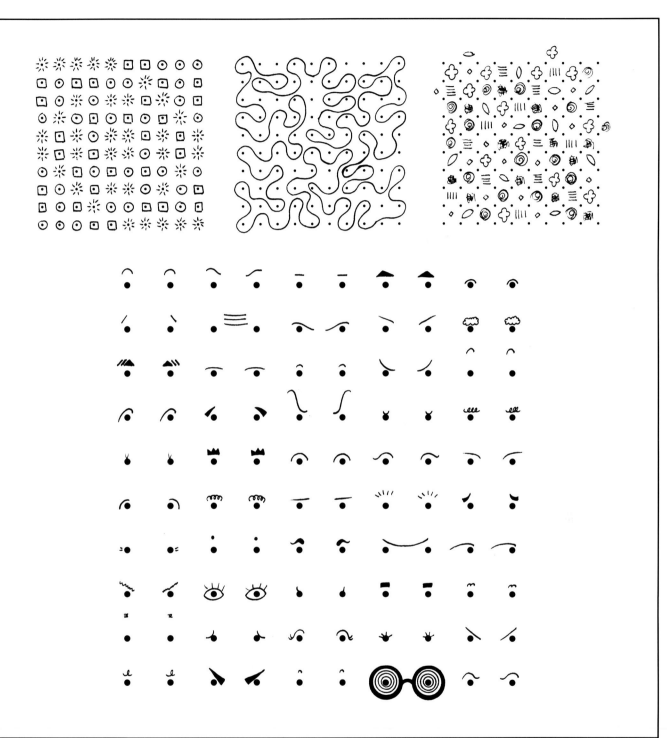

10

1. FRANK CASTALDI
2. JILLIAN MYERS
3. AMI LACHER
4. DALE SUTPHEN
5. MISSY WILLIAMS
6. CYNTHIA PRADO
7. DALE SUTPHEN
8. BEVERLEY PERKIN
9. TRILBY WILDE
10. ELEANOR HARNICK

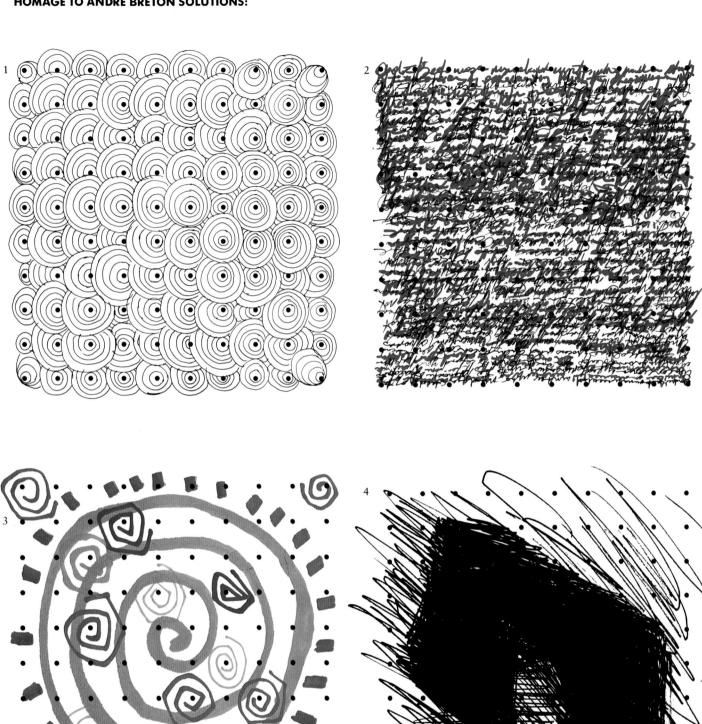

5

6
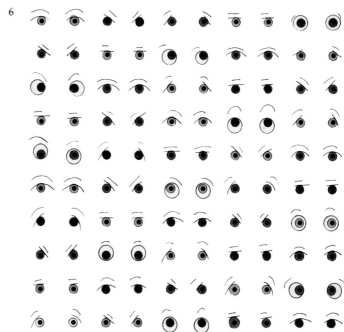

7

8

1. KIMBERLY DESCETTO
2. DONNA ELLIOTT
3. ESTELLE FLEISCHER
4. JENNIFER GRIMBILAS
5. ERIC C. KING
6. KIMBERLY D. SCHEREMETA
7. DEBBIE GUY
8. JON DUEDE

PART 2. ILLUSTRATION EXERCISES

The following illustration assignments are structured to facilitate the discovery and refinement of artistic style as a means of personal expression. Experimentation and risk taking continue to be encouraged, enhanced by an additional emphasis on craft and skill. These attributes, combined with a conceptual approach to problem solving, inevitably result in the effective visual communication that is an integral part of competent illustration.

The illustration problems were assigned in the form of written instructions only—no assignment sheets or other materials were included. In this section of the book, therefore, each problem's instructions and analysis are presented alone, with the corresponding solution art following directly thereafter.

WORLD RECORD PROBLEM:

Illustrate a world record of any fact, statistic, deed, or achievement, in any field or subject area. Consider the natural world, outer space, bizarre and outrageous stunts, challenging exploits, great sports accomplishments, or occurrences that are ridiculous, provocative, or shocking.

1

THREE WHOLE LEMONS EATEN IN 15.3 SECONDS

2

THE LARGEST SCARECROW: 73′5¾″

3

THE TALLEST FLAGPOLE: 299′7″

1. TRISTAN A. ELWELL
2. FRANCESA PELAGGI
3. DREW BISHOP

1

THE LARGEST DRUM EVER CONSTRUCTED

2

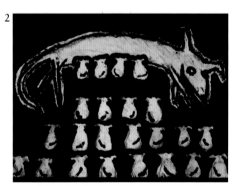

THE LARGEST LITTER OF PUPPIES: 23

3

THE LARGEST BUBBLE BLOWN:
22 INCHES IN DIAMETER

4

SMALLEST KNOWN SHARK: 5.9 INCHES

5

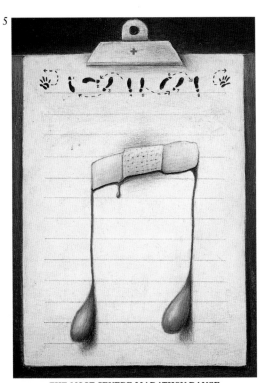

**THE MOST SEVERE MARATHON DANCE:
5,148 HOURS, 28.5 MINUTES**

6

THE LARGEST CUCUMBER GROWN: 59 POUNDS

7

**THE FASTEST TIME FOR TYING SIX
BOY SCOUT KNOTS: 8.1 SECONDS**

8

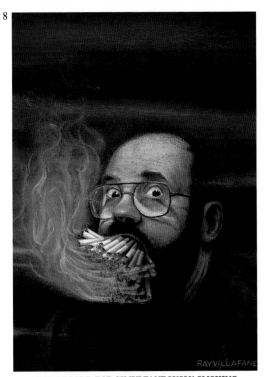

**THE RECORD FOR SIMULTANEOUSLY SMOKING
CIGARETTES: 140 CIGARETTES FOR 5 MINUTES.**

THE MOST TATTOOS: 5,473

THE LONGEST FREIGHT TRAIN: 4 MILES

THE SMALLEST BIRD IS THE BEE HUMMINGBIRD: 2.24 INCHES

THE LONGEST MOUSTACHE: 110.5 IN.

THE LARGEST RABBIT: 25 POUNDS

THE LONGEST DISTANCE FOR A HUMAN FIRED FROM A CANNON: 175 FT.

THE HEAVIEST TOMATO GROWN: 7¾ POUNDS

Create an illustration of a New York City landscape. The point of view can be your own or anyone (or anything) else's. Consider the possibilities: You can depict New York from the vantage point of an insect on the ground, whose vista is limited, or of a pigeon flying above the city with an unlimited view; you can portray the city through the eyes of a well-groomed, well-fed French poodle, or through the unfocused eyes of a drug addict. On the back of your artwork, write a short paragraph explaining the point of view of your New York City landscape.

Use the following definition as a guide: "Landscape: (a) a picture representing a view of natural scenery; (b) a portion of the land that the eye can comprehend in a single view; (c) vista; prospect."

Choose one of three horizontal sizes: 11×14 inches, 14×17 inches, or 16×20 inches. There are no limitations on the use of color or media.

Analysis: The key to the problem lies in the choice of a specific point of view. Because the choices are limitless, and because there are endless opportunities to manipulate the vantage point as it relates to the scale of human beings and/or of the surrounding landscape, the illustrator must choose carefully to communicate a particular emotional and visual view.

NEW YORK CITY LANDSCAPE SOLUTIONS:

DANIELLE IMPERIALE

PAUL DINOVO

JIM MC NEILL

SEAN DALTON

NEW YORK CITY LANDSCAPE SOLUTIONS:

TRISTAN A. ELWELL

SANDRO RODORIGO

MARK ELLIOT

PHILLIP SINGER

JOE DANISI

SCOTT LESIAK

RICHARD PILOCO

175

NEW YORK CITY LANDSCAPE SOLUTIONS:

VINCENT JOVIC

PHILIPPE LARDY

JASON SEDER

DAVID WACHTENHEIM

BRIAN CLYNE

CHRISTOPHER SPINELLI

LAURA SMITH

SOUND PROBLEM II:

Choose one or more sounds and translate this auditory experience into visual terms; that is, portray the sounds pictorially. Keep in mind that sounds can represent emotions ranging from love and comfort to violence and fear; they can be humorous and joyous as well as menacing and unpleasant. Any image that you feel represents a sound may be depicted. Your illustration can be abstract or representational.

Maximum size is 14 × 17 inches. There are no limitations on color or media. On the back of your assignment sheet, write a title explaining your sound.

Analysis: This problem is an extension of Sound Problem I (see page 128), except here there is only one problem to be solved, and the sounds must be chosen by the illustrator. Unlike Sound Problem I, here a narrative approach is encouraged and pictorial concerns are emphasized.

John Ramhorst 87

1

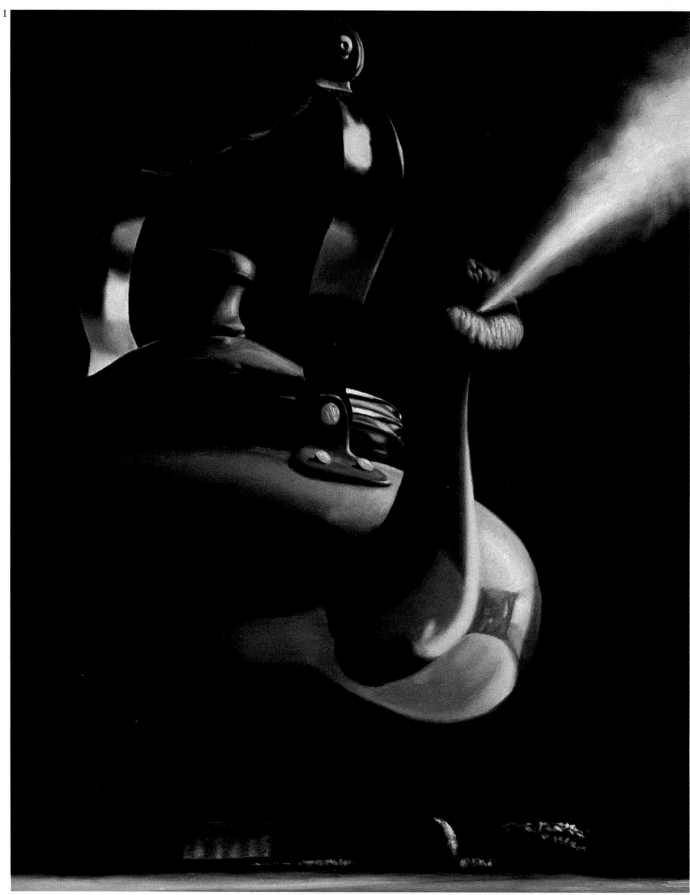

WHISTLING TEA KETTLE

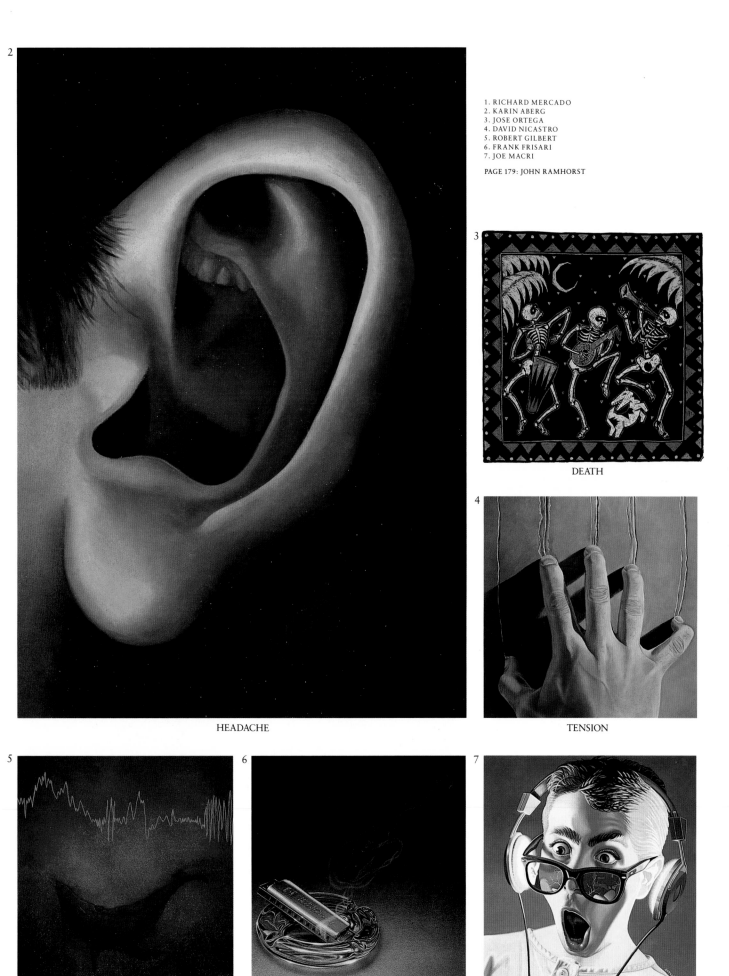

1. RICHARD MERCADO
2. KARIN ABERG
3. JOSE ORTEGA
4. DAVID NICASTRO
5. ROBERT GILBERT
6. FRANK FRISARI
7. JOE MACRI

PAGE 179: JOHN RAMHORST

DEATH

HEADACHE

TENSION

DEEP VOICES

HOT TUNE

VOLUME

SOUND SOLUTIONS:

1

SUBWAY

2

CONDUCTING

3

AIR RAID

4

MUZAK

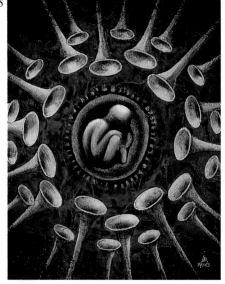

5

UNKNOWING

6

PIN DROPPING

1. KARIN ABERG
2. KYMBERLY YOUNG
3. RANDALL SAUCHUCK
4. GEORGE PORFIRIS
5. JEFF MUHS
6. DAVE LAWSON
7. ANDREA J. ELSTON

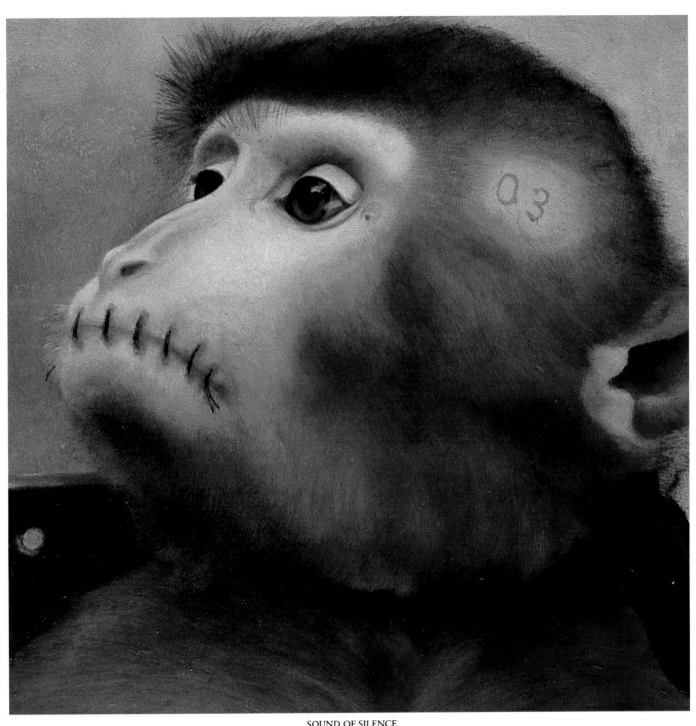

SOUND OF SILENCE

NUMBER ELEVEN PROBLEM:

Transform the number eleven into an illustration as a personal expression of yourself. Use numerals, letters, metaphors, symbolism, or any other approach you find appropriate.

Image size should be 6×9 inches. There are no limitations on the use of color or media.

Analysis: The intention here is to move away from ordinary imagery to the world of pictorial exploration, where both concept and execution are of high importance. The final solution must solve the given problem of being recognizable as the number eleven while at the same time transcending the number's literal meaning.

NUMBER ELEVEN SOLUTIONS:

Utilizing a graphic element, such as a number, and interpreting it pictorially defines this problem in a unique way, and is the starting point for producing original work.

PREVIOUS PAGE: TRISTAN A. ELWELL   ADAM SCHECTER

186

LISA MC LEOD

MICHAEL P. VISOSKY

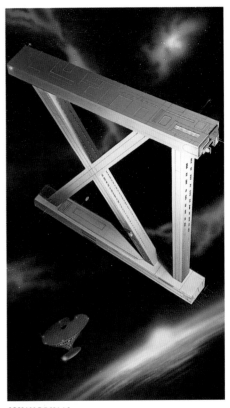

JOHAN DE HAAS

GEORGE J. WINTER

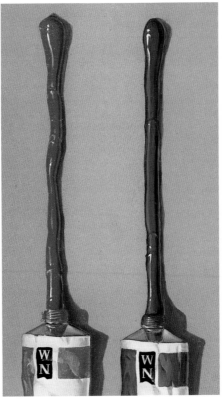

JOHN MANDATO

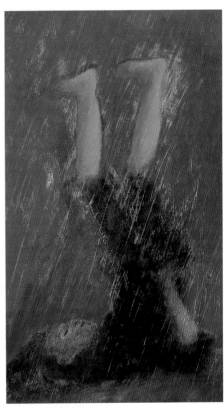

EMILY MARTINDALE

NUMBER ELEVEN SOLUTIONS:

In a problem such as this, any number could be substituted with the same results. These solutions show the results of working with the number ten.

SEAN DALTON

PHILLIP SINGER

ELIZABETH MILLER

SANDRO RODORIGO

189

CREDITS

PAGE 56

COLUMN 1.
1. MISSY WILLIAMS
2. HSIU-YUN LUO
3. KARIN HENRIKSON
4. IP KWOK PO BOCO
5. JEFF SCHULZ
6. MARIA RAMBO

COLUMN 2.
1. KIM C. BARRES
2. KIM C. BARRES
3. PAULA DI MARCO
4. HANOCH PIVEN
5. BIRGITTE FJORD
6. PAULA DI MARCO

COLUMN 3.
1. KATE PALLADINO
2. SHARON HAREL
3. JULIE CLARKE
4. SHARON HAREL
5. SHARON HAREL
6. CHRIS GARCIA

PAGE 57

COLUMN 1.
1. STEPHEN CANNATO
2. MELISSA COOKE
3. PAGE EDWARDS
4. SHARON HAREL
5. ROB CARTER
6. DAVID QUASHA

COLUMN 2.
1. DAVID QUASHA
2. PAGE EDWARDS
3. KOBY CAULY
4. JOYCE MACEK
5. JOHN LUTTROPP
6. JONATHAN REED

COLUMN 3.
1. IP KWOK PO BOCO
2. KATE PALLADINO
3. EVA MARIE PATURZOK
4. JEFFREY D. SUPPER
5. IP KWOK PO BOCO
6. RICHARD BRIGGS

PAGE 58

COLUMN 1.
1. IP KWOK PO BOCO
2. AYAKO HOSONO
3. JEFF SCHULZ
4. JEFF SCHULZ
5. BETTE COWLES
6. LINDA WELLS

COLUMN 2.
1. IP KWOK PO BOCO
2. KARIN HENRIKSON
3. SARAH JANE PATENT
4. CHRISTOPHER JOHN ROCCO
5. ROGER SCHINKLER
6. SHARON HAREL

COLUMN 3.
1. IP KWOK PO BOCO
2. JEFF SCHULZ
3. KIM C. BARRES
4. PAULA DIMARCO
5. SARAH JANE PATENT
6. DAVID QUASHA

PAGE 59

COLUMN 1.
1. KIM C. BARRES
2. VALERIE
3. SHARON HAREL
4. EVA MARIE PATURZO
5. BETTE COWLES
6. JOHN LUTTROPP

COLUMN 2.
1. DAVID QUASHA
2. YU-ZHOU LUO
3. LISA MAZUR
4. HANOCH PIVEN
5. SARAH JANE PATENT
6. JONATHAN REED

COLUMN 3.
1. AYAKO HOSONO
2. AYAKO HOSONO
3. RICHARD BRIGGS
4. AYAKO HOSONO
5. IP KWOK PO BOCO
6. RICHARD BRIGGS

PAGE 60

COLUMN 1.
1. MARIA RAMBO
2. WENDY SCHIMPF
3. SHARON HAREL
4. BETTE COWLES
5. IP KWOK PO BOCO
6. ROGER SCHINKLER

COLUMN 2.
1. MELISSA COOKE
2. PAGE EDWARDS
3. GLENN RUGA
4. WENDY SCHIMPF
5. ROGER SCHINKLER
6. KOBY CAULY

COLUMN 3.
1. JEFF SCHULZ
2. RICHARD BRIGGS
3. WENDY SCHIMPF
4. IP KWOK PO BOCO
5. WENDY SCHIMPF
6. JOHN LUTTROPP

PAGE 61

COLUMN 1.
1. EVA MARIE PATURZO
2. IP KWOK PO BOCO
3. JOHN LUTTROPP
4. KIM C. BARRES
5. SHARON HAREL
6. STEPHEN CANNATO

COLUMN 2.
1. AYAKO HOSONO
2. JEFF SCHULZ
3. DAVID QUASHA
4. IP KWOK PO BOCO
5. HANOCH PIVEN
6. JAVIER CASTILLO

COLUMN 3.
1. DAVID QUASHA
2. HANOCH PIVEN
3. JEFF SCHULZ
4. CHRIS KLEIN
5. SOFIA PAIVA RAPOSO
6. MARIA BELFIORE

PAGE 62

COLUMN 1.
1. CHRIS KLEIN
2. MELISSA COOKE
3. MELISSA COOKE
4. PAULA DIMARCO
5. ANITA GRACIN

COLUMN 2.
1. DAVID QUASHA
2. CHRIS KLEIN
3. ERIC C. KING
4. CHRISTOPHER JOHN ROCCO
5. CARIN POMBO

COLUMN 3.
1. MELISSA COOKE
2. MICHAEL S. VASSALLO
3. LISA MAZUR
4. KOBY CAULY
5. JOANNA WIECEK

PAGE 63

COLUMN 1.
1. MARIA CAMILLERI
2. RICHARD BRIGGS
3. STEPHEN CANNATO
4. MIRANDA MUSHFIQA NG
5. CHRISTOPHER JOHN ROCCO

COLUMN 2.
1. ROB CARTER
2. PAGE EDWARDS
3. CHRISTOPHER JOHN ROCCO
4. MATTHEW ENOCK
5. YU-ZHOU LUO

COLUMN 3.
1. ROB CARTER
2. EVA MARIE PATURZO
3. SARAH DEJAHNETTE
4. JOHN LUTTROPP
5. CHRISTOPHER JOHN ROCCO

BACK JACKET

COLUMN 1.
1. IP KWOK PO BOCO
2. PAGE EDWARDS
3. VALERIE LAUSEN
4. SHARON HAREL
5. HANOCH PIVEN

COLUMN 2.
1. SARAH JANE PATENT
2. KIM C. BARRES
3. JEFF SCHULZ
4. MIKKO MERONEN
5. JEFFREY D. SUPPER

COLUMN 3.
1. IP KWOK PO BOCO
2. IP KWOK PO BOCO
3. JEFFREY D. SUPPER
4. IP KWOK PO BOCO
5. EVA MARIE PATURZO

COLUMN 4.
1. HSIU-YUN LUO
2. HANOCH PIVEN
3. IP KWOK PO BOCO
4. PAGE EDWARDS
5. MELISSA COOKE

COLUMN 5.
1. AYAKO HOSONO
2. JOHN LUTTROPP
3. WENDY SCHIMPF
4. IP KWOK PO BOCO
5. JEFF SCHULZ

Edited by Paul Lukas
Graphic production by Hector Campbell
Set in 12-point Century Old Style